Laughter in the Shadows

Laughter in the Shadows
A CIA MEMOIR

Stuart E. Methven

NAVAL INSTITUTE PRESS
Annapolis, Maryland

Naval Institute Press
291 Wood Road
Annapolis, MD 21402

Library of Congress Cataloging-in-Publication Data
Methven, Stuart E.
  Laughter in the shadows : a CIA memoir / Stuart E. Methven.
      p. cm.
  Includes index.
  ISBN 978-1-59114-517-2 (alk. paper)
  1. Methven, Stuart E. 2. Intelligence officers—United States—Biography. 3. United
States. Central Intelligence Agency—Officials and employees—Biography. I. Title.
JK468.I6M48 2008
  327.12730092—dc22
  [B]
                                                              2008043950

Printed in the United States of America on acid-free paper

14 13 12 11 10 09 08   9 8 7 6 5 4 3 2
First printing

This manuscript has been reviewed by the CIA to assist the author in eliminating
classified information; however, that review neither constitutes CIA authentication of
factual material nor implies CIA endorsement of the author's views.

Photographs are from the author's personal collection.

To my immediate family: Laurie, Kent, Gray, and Megan, who lived through *Laughter* in both Asia and Africa, and to their spouses, Kris, Denise, Terri, and Rusty, and to their progeny, Marcus, Page, Joey, Jessica, Mike, Brian, Amber, and Kendall

And to my devoted wife Nicole, who was part of the African equation and provided steadfast support and affection in getting me to finish this book

CONTENTS

ACKNOWLEDGMENTS

—⁂—

I would like to thank my friends and colleagues, Tom Ahern and Ed George, the latter particularly for his input into the book's introduction.

I am also indebted to my brother Don, now deceased, who helped correct and provide support, and to his family, especially my nephews David and Mike, who carried on with support for the book after my brother's death.

Finally, I thank Jerrold and Leona Schecter, my patient and supportive literary agents and longtime friends, and the Naval Institute Press for the book's unique cover and their vote of confidence in publishing *Laughter in the Shadows*.

INTRODUCTION

And yet—it's rather curious, you know, this sort of life! I do wonder what
can have happened to me! When I used to read fairy tales, I fancied
that kind of thing never happened, and now here I am in the middle
of one!

There ought to be a book written about me, that there ought!
And when I grow up, I'll write one.

—LEWIS CARROLL, *Alice in Wonderland*

—\\\\\\—

In a period of American history that seems to abound in startling ironies and
melodramas, perhaps none is as striking as that of the Central Intelligence
Agency (CIA). Here is an organization, dedicated to anonymity, that suddenly
became the most widely and sensationally publicized secret institution in history.

It was incredible, the stuff of comedy and tragedy, unexpected and improbable, ludicrous and grave. In the catalogue of the CIA's alleged misdeeds, there was
a hint of some cosmic mind at work behind the scenes. The scheme to destroy
or denigrate Castro, sinister in its intent, slapstick in its results, or "stemming
the tide" in Southeast Asia with bands of ragged tribesmen, ideal in conception,
bloody in conclusion.

Make no mistake about it: even with the CIA's flaws, the Central Intelligence
Agency has much to be proud of. In its early years, there was probably no other
federal agency with a comparable level of talent and expertise in so many different
and often arcane fields. No other agency was less bureaucratic and hidebound. No
other agency was more demanding or tolerant of its people.

The results were remarkable. Out of an improbable mix of high purposes
and low methods, cloistered intellectuals and daring adventurers, opportunists
and idealists, bureaucrats and innovators, the Agency fashioned one of the most
efficient, effective, and responsive organizations in the U.S. government.

The damage inflicted on the CIA later by unwanted publicity forced it to
retrench and consequently to lose much of its independent spirit. Yet, even with
the unfrocking of its main opponent, the KGB (the Soviet Union's Committee
for State Security), the Agency still has a formidably complex task trying to find
coherence and predictability in a crazy-quilt world tattered and torn at by insur-
gents, terrorists, war lords, and religious fanatics.

This book is about the early, more heady days of the CIA. It is the story of essentially conventional people in a chimerical, yet precarious world, written by an operations officer who was part of it.

The experience was almost addictive. Those of us involved might not approve of or fully comprehend everything that was happening, but we couldn't tear ourselves away. The constant sense of wonder led us to raise questions but left us unsure about the answers.

The characters in this book are real, although names have been changed to protect those still guarding their cover. Locales where covert engagements may still be running have been disguised.

If at times the book pokes fun at the Agency, it is not to discredit it. The demarcation between the rational and the fanciful has never been well defined, and one may very well have thought he was in one state without realizing he had crossed into the other. This is why even the best-intentioned clandestine operations appear tragicomic in their tail-chasing frenzy.

This book tries to capture that early spirit of the CIA's finest hour, when it almost self-destructed, yet left its brightest trail.

PART I
The Beginning

Bear with me,—and let me go on, and tell my story my own way:—or, if I should seem now and then to trifle upon the road,—or should sometimes put on a fool's cap with a bell to it . . . don't fly off,—but, rather, courteously give me credit for a little more wisdom than appears upon my outside.

—LAURENCE STERNE
The Life and Opinions of Tristram Shandy

CHAPTER 1: **Enlistment**

A mherst College, cloistered in the center of rural New England, was alive with the rumor that a "general" would be the 1951 commencement speaker. The general seemed an odd choice because Amherst had no military tradition, although the college had been named after Gen. Lord Jeffrey Amherst, who, as the Amherst College song notes, was "a soldier of the king," who conquered all the Indians in this wild country (by offering them smallpox-infected blankets).

The commencement speaker was Walter Bedell ("Beetle") Smith, Gen. Dwight D. Eisenhower's chief of staff during World War II. General Smith had recently been named director of the Central Intelligence Agency (CIA), a recently established government organization whose functions were as yet undefined.

During the spring of 1951, recruiters from the new organization had been combing Ivy League campuses for "bright young men." Amherst College actually had more "Gentlemen C" students than Phi Beta Kappa scholars, but the CIA recruiters stopped by anyway. I had just completed my history thesis on "Espionage in the American Civil War," describing America's first intelligence organization (the Pinkerton Detective Agency), highlighting exploits of Union and Confederate female spies, and citing the origins of aerial surveillance operations (i.e., observation balloons floating over the Petersburg salient), and I was certain my thesis would impress the recruiters.

I was surprised by several of the odd questions put to me by the interviewers: What did I think about the Abraham Lincoln Brigade? (I said I had been impressed by Ingrid Bergman in *For Whom the Bell Tolls*.) How did I feel about homosexuals? (I said there weren't any in my fraternity.) The only question I found relevant was whether or not I had scruples about "reading other people's mail." (I said I thought it might be interesting; then quickly added, "if it was for a good cause.")

When the questions were finished, I handed over a copy of my thesis about intelligence activities during the American Civil War. One of them glanced briefly at the title and tossed it into his briefcase. Then they stood up, shook my hand, and said they would be in touch.

A week later an envelope arrived, postmarked Washington, D.C. No return address. The letter inside bore the seal of the Central Intelligence Agency. It contained an offer of employment as a CIA operations officer, Grade GS-7 (the civil service equivalent of a first lieutenant), salary $7,500 per annum.

I was so elated with the offer I almost forgot to read further. The last paragraph stated that the offer of employment was contingent on a "security clearance," a process that required a period of six months to complete. To expedite the clearance, I was asked to fill out the enclosed thirty-seven-page Personal History Statement.

Six months. My earlier elation had been premature. I couldn't wait six months for a "clearance." I had just gotten married and needed a job after I graduated. My GI Bill benefits had run out, and a new addition to the family was due in November.

I would have to postpone my dream of joining the world's "second oldest profession." I accepted a job as a management trainee with the U.S. Rubber Company in Naugatuck, Connecticut. No security clearance required.

—◊—

Naugatuck is the rubber capital of America. Vulcanization was invented in Naugatuck by Charles Goodyear, whose legacy to the town was the cloud of burning rubber that hung over it and seeped into the pores of its inhabitants.

After a brief training period, I was assigned to the Gumshoe Department as an assistant foreman. In Naugatuck, Connecticut, "gumshoes" aren't "private eyes," like Sam Spade and Philip Marlow. In Naugatuck gumshoes are "rubbers"—not Sheiks or Trojans sold under drugstore counters, but elastic protectors that keep shoes from getting wet.

A hundred and thirty-two women and fourteen men worked in the Gumshoe Department. Every day, for eight hours, they stood or sat in front of a conveyor belt, placing soft rubber cutouts on passing shoe lasts. The last worker on the line stuck the L.L. Bean or U.S. Keds label on the back of the gumshoe and placed the last on a rack, which, when filled, would be rolled off to the vulcanizing ovens.

As a junior foreman, I wasn't given too much responsibility. The general foreman and his line supervisors ran things the way they always had before management forced a college trainee on them.

At first, the supervisors ignored me, or tried to, anyway. After a while, however, once they realized I had no intention of interfering with their established routines, they accepted me and ultimately gave me small tasks to perform, such as filling out quality control sheets, checking production figures, and dealing with the union steward.

Six months of watching the endless parade of gumshoes coming off the conveyors and listening to the complaints of the union steward bored me. I also became frustrated with the realization that I was cut off from the rubber company managers, who obviously forgot their trainees once they disgorged them into the factory.

To relieve the boredom, I resorted to the suggestion box. My first suggestion was a proposal for a new line of gumshoe to be called La Cache. One heel of each pair of La Cache would be hollowed out for a secret compartment to hide billets-doux and "mad money."

The La Cache suggestion generated no response, and I submitted another suggestion for a new line, the Firefly, which featured fluorescent-coated heels and toe-caps. I pointed out that this line would be popular with joggers, hikers, and night-walkers as a "revolutionary stride" in shoe safety. Several weeks later I was advised that the Firefly suggestion had been forwarded to the Research Department "for further study." As with the La Cache suggestion, however, nothing came of it.

Increasingly frustrated, I asked for a transfer to the Special Products Department, where state-of-the-art golf balls, odorless diapers, and art deco birth control devices were being developed.

Unlike my contributions to the suggestion box, the transfer request attracted management's attention, and I was summoned to the office of the director of personnel. The director was thumbing through my folder when I arrived. He motioned for me to sit down, closed my folder, and asked me why, with such a promising future in the Gumshoe Department, I wanted a transfer. I was about to reply, but he held up his hand.

"I am going to tell you something that is completely confidential," he said. "Your general foreman, Frank Smith, has decided to retire at the end of the year. There is a very good chance you will be named to take his place. This would be quite a step up for a young foreman who has been on the job less than a year. It normally takes from eight to ten years to even be considered for a general foreman's job, and it would be a great opportunity for you. This is what you should keep in mind before asking for a transfer."

Frank hadn't told me he was going to retire, but then, the general foreman had never been very communicative, particularly with his junior assistant. The director of personnel was right. It would be a big step up. The general foreman sat behind a glassed-in partition cushioned from the clamor of the throbbing conveyors and clanking shoe racks. He spent much of his time attending management meetings and quality control conferences. And most important, he didn't have to put up with the union steward. I decided to withdraw my transfer request and wait out Frank's retirement.

Having now been assured of a more promising future, I became more relaxed in my foreman's role. I worried less about production quotas and quality control and tried not to let the union steward get under my skin. I didn't succeed, however, and ironically, it was because of the union steward that I never got to sit behind that glassed-in partition.

The big annual event in Naugatuck is the fourth of July picnic. The entire factory shut down, and, as if by grand design, the cloud of Naugahyde lifted for the day to let the sun filter through. The entire town either went to the picnic or took the chartered U.S. Rubber train to New York for the Yankee–Red Sox baseball game.

At the park entrance, a HAPPY FOURTH OF JULY! banner was stretched between two oak trees, planted fifty years earlier by an enterprising city council. The park inside resembled a Norman Rockwell *Saturday Evening Post* cover, with concession stands draped in red, white, and blue bunting offering foot-long hot dogs and frosted steins of "Naugabrew." Picnickers bit at bobbing apples in galvanized washtubs on their way to compete in the one-legged sack races, mud wrestling, and the tug-of-war contest. Beer barrel polkas boomed from loudspeakers in the trees, drowning out the speeches of the mayor and factory manager. Parents danced the do-si-dos to the accompaniment of fiddlers and stomp-and-holler callers, while their teenaged offspring necked in the back of the family Studebaker.

My wife, Joy, and I felt good as we walked down the hill to the park, listening to the staccato of ladyfinger firecrackers and the thumping of tubas in the distance. Inside the park we bobbed for apples and pitched a game of horseshoes. After a picnic lunch, we went to watch the softball game between the Gumshoe Roosters and the Canvas Mallards.

It was during the bottom half of the fifth inning that Ray Mengacci strolled over.

Ray Mengacci was the union steward for Local #21, United Rubber Workers of America. He strutted around the factory as if he was the reincarnation of the American Federation of Laborer's founder, Samuel Gompers.

When he came into the Gumshoe Department, he made it a point to ignore me and go directly over to the conveyor belts. He worked the conveyor lines like a Chicago ward heeler, calling out to workers by their first names, asking about their families, and inquiring if they weren't working too hard.

Ray liked being on stage, and I knew his routine by heart. He would begin by walking over to one of the conveyor belts, where he'd take up a position behind one of the workers, always picking one he knew to be nervous and excitable.

Ray would then stand behind her with his arms crossed, looking over her shoulder as she placed the rubber cutouts on passing shoe lasts. With the union steward standing behind her looking over her shoulder, she would invariably become rattled and begin putting the cutouts on the last crooked or upside down until eventually she would start missing lasts altogether, which would cause her to sob and break into tears. This would give Ray his cue. He would march over to the end of the conveyor belt and throw the switch, shutting down the line.

Once the conveyor belt had clanked to a stop, Ray would step back and assume a Mussolini pose, with his arms crossed and his chin jutting out. Then he would begin his steward's litany:

"Fellow workers! Look at poor Nell crying!"

The workers on the line would all turn to look at Nell.

"Why is she crying? Because that college-boy foreman"—pointing in my direction—"has ratcheted up the speed of your conveyor!"

The workers would turn and look at me.

"Why does he speed up the conveyor? I'll tell you why. By increasing your production and turning out more and more gumshoes, he looks good to his bosses.

"But this time he won't get away with it. I am going to bring this up with the Grievance Committee, and they will take my complaint to the plant superintendant, who will order your boy foreman to slow the conveyor and stop running the Gumshoe Department like a sweatshop!

"And Nell won't have to cry anymore!"

Ray would pat Nell on the back, raise his hands over his head like a victorious boxer, and leave. Ray was the hero; I, the hissed villain.

Sometimes, on the way out, when no one was looking, Ray would wink at me.

When I saw Ray coming toward us while we were watching the softball game, I wondered what the Italian bugbear was up to. Ray slapped me on the back like we were old friends, then introduced himself to Joy, turning on the Mediterranean charm that kept getting him reelected as union steward.

I decided to ignore Ray and turned back to watch the game. I had little trouble overhearing Ray as he invited Joy for a homemade spaghetti dinner one evening, adding that she could bring her husband along. Ray was probably aware I was listening, because he quickly lowered his voice so I could catch only parts of what he was saying about "your husband's problem . . . harassing workers . . . making women cry," and then, raising his voice, he added, "If he doesn't change his ways, he would probably end up in the vulcanizer . . . come out shriveled up like a prune!"

Ray had gone too far and I turned to confront him. Unfortunately, he was already walking away after telling Joy he was "only kidding" about the vulcanizer and not to forget his invitation for a spaghetti dinner.

Ray had succeeded in ruining the picnic, having described me to Joy as a slave-driving Simon Legree and a candidate for the vulcanizer. I had already heard tales circulating around the mill and local bars about vulcanizer "accidents" and had no trouble imagining the satanic grin on Ray's face as I was wheeled into my fiery immolation.

I decided to leave the picnic early before the display of fireworks. When we got home, I went straight to the basement and began rummaging through the boxes we still hadn't unpacked until, at the bottom of one of them, I found what I was looking for: a fat manila envelope containing a thirty-seven-page questionnaire.

The next three nights I spent filling out the questionnaire, calling my parents for details and dates of my early bed-wetting habits, childhood illnesses, school records, and so forth. My father's memory was as porous as mine, but my mother was an inveterate pack rat and still had my old vaccination records, school report cards, and certificates of Boy Scout merit badges.

I filled out the thirty-seven pages, signed at the bottom attesting that "all the information was true and correct to the best of my knowledge," and sent it off to Washington.

Two weeks later a telegram arrived requesting that I come to Washington for an interview. It didn't inquire why it had taken me over a year to fill out the questionnaire.

The sign on the anchor-fence at 1410 E Street read Naval Research Facility. A guard at the gate pointed to the brick mansion with white pillars at the end of a circular driveway. It looked like an antebellum plantation manor. A receptionist sat at a desk under a large chandelier that hung from a flaking gilt ceiling. A spiral staircase, where southern suitors had awaited the descent of their Scarletts, led to the second floor where my interview was to take place.

My interviewer was a bald man with Coke-bottle glasses. He motioned for me to sit down, offering a cup of coffee while he finished looking thorough the folder containing my questionnaire. He closed the folder, leaned forward, and said he had only one question: "How do you feel about jumping out of an airplane?"

I was caught off guard by what was probably a trick question. I remembered a war story about D-day. A paratrooper had got caught on a church steeple, leaving him hanging helplessly, prey for German snipers. I told the interviewer that parachute jumping sounded exciting. I didn't add that it beat being vulcanized.

He jotted something in my folder and came around the desk to shake my hand. "Welcome to the CIA!"

He told me I had been selected for a "high priority" Agency program. My clearance was being expedited, and I could count on "coming on board" within sixty days. When I returned to Naugatuck, I didn't tell anyone I would be leaving because I didn't want to burn that bridge to the general foreman's job if the CIA clearance didn't come through. A month later I received a telegram advising me that my clearance had come through. I was to report to Washington as soon as possible.

The rubber company personnel director couldn't understand why I was passing up the chance to become a general foreman. I pointed to the "DON'T DIE ON THIRD!" sign over his desk and said that third base for me was the Gumshoe Department, and I needed to move on.

The Gumshoe Department gave me a farewell party. Nell cried "for old times' sake," and I proposed a toast to my good friends in the department, including the union steward, adding that "every college boy needs a Ray Mengacci in his life!" I winked at Ray.

We packed up the Pontiac, strapped five-month-old Laurie into the car seat, took a last breath of Naugahyde, and headed off for Washington.

When I arrived at the E Street entrance, I noticed for the first time the more imposing Department of State building across the street. With its Italian marble front, spacious lobby, and queue of limousines in the driveway, it stood in dignified contrast to its upstart neighbor hiding behind the Potemkin front of a "Naval Research" facility.

The same receptionist handed me a clipboard of forms to fill out. Most were routine forms having to do with bank deposits, health insurance, the credit union, and who to advise in case of death. The last form was a Secrecy Agreement binding me not to reveal my CIA employment to anyone and never to speak or write about any of my activities in the CIA without permission.

I balked at the monastic vow binding me to forever sheathe my pen and seal my lips. Even Alice was able to recount her adventures after she emerged from the rabbit hole. I bit my tongue and signed.

I handed in the form and went down the hall to be given a polygraph and a physical exam, and at the end of the day, I was sworn in.

CHAPTER 2: **Training**

Think back: We all became spies as children: that's the only way we know to make sense of the world.

—AMANDA CROSS, *An Imperfect Spy*

The new recruits boarded the Agency's Blue Bird bus for the trip across town to the training site, an amphitheater in a park near the Potomac River. The amphitheater, set behind a clump of trees, was barely visible from the road. The chimes of the Netherlands carillon were the only sounds breaking the silence.

Guards checked our newly issued badges on the way in, trying in vain to match photos with faces. Inside we filed into an auditorium, our classroom for the two-month orientation course.

First, however, we were given our pseudonyms. Every Agency officer is christened with a pseudonym, the alter ego he will carry with him throughout his career. He will be paid in pseudonym, cited in dispatches in pseudonym, reprimanded in pseudonym, decorated in pseudonym, and retired or terminated in pseudonym.

Pseudonyms are selected from a list of names on file in Registry. One officer in our group didn't like the pseudonym he had been given, Carl RAINTREE, because he thought it implied Apache ancestry. When he asked for another pseudonym, he was told a pseudonym could not be changed unless it was "compromised." The officer then deliberately left his pay slip with his RAINTREE pseudonym out on his desk. The slip was discovered and turned in by the night security guard. RAINTREE was reprimanded, given a security violation, and assigned a new pseudonym: Jerome P. TWADDLEDUCK.

We were given the outline of a cover story we were to use with outsiders. The cover story, a fable woven from half truths, was in the early 1950s a device designed to deflect Russian KGB agents in their attempts to identify CIA officers. In practice, however, the cover story confounded friends and neighbors more than it did the Russians.

My cover story, which I laid on with my next-door neighbor, was that I was an analyst with the Defense Department. Unfortunately, as it turned out, my neighbor was truly employed by the Defense Department, and he responded to my story by asking me to join his car pool to the Pentagon. When I begged off, citing odd working hours, he asked me to meet him for lunch in the Pentagon cafeteria and again I had to put him off. He finally saw through my "Defense analyst" charade and resigned himself to having a "spook" as his neighbor.

My relatives, particularly my in-laws, were not as understanding. They became convinced, as I kept changing cover stories with each new assignment, that I couldn't hold down a steady job.

The Curriculum

Long before Moses sent spies into Canaan, Sumerian rulers were sending out agents to bedevil their opponents. There seems in fact to have been no period in history during which secret agents have not played a part in political and military affairs.

—ERIC AMBLER, *Epitaph for a Spy*

The course opened with a history of the world's "second oldest profession." The earliest recorded agent operations, documented in the Dead Sea Scrolls, were run by Moses, who recruited "agents" to reconnoiter routes to walk across the Red Sea. Stick-figure cave scratchings of spear-carrying warriors illustrated prehistoric paramilitary operations. Julius Caesar was extolled for creating the first military intelligence (G-2) branch, which was instrumental in his conquest of Gaul. His Praetorian successors, however, were faulted for serious "intelligence failures" in underestimating the capabilities of the barbarians at the gate.

The Espionage Hall of Fame inductees included Nathan Hale, Benedict Arnold, Mata Hari, and Kim Philby.

My Oscar for training films went to "The Tawny Pipit," starring two rara avis pipits, surveillance targets of a team of ornithologists. The two bird-watchers suffered the damp cold and biting winds of the Scottish highlands for over a year, recording the feeding and sexual habits of the pipits. The ornithologists even ran a bugging operation, slipping two egg-shaped microphones into the nest. As an audio operation, it was a failure, however, because the pipits disdainfully pecked out the "bugs" and dropped them into the bog.

Sessions on "tradecraft" covered recruitment of agents (beware of "dangles" and "doubles"), clandestine meetings (don't arrange rendezvous "under the old oak tree," which may have perished from elm rot), danger signals (avoid using the upside-down "For Rent" sign in the window, which the cleaning woman probably will probably put back right side up), and dead drops (don't use air conditioners, which are too often sent out for repairs with the coded message inside).

The course lasted four weeks. When it was over, eighteen of us were taken aside and told we were being sent to The Farm for a six-month "special training" course. We were to "pack light" and be ready to leave the following Monday.

The Farm

Lest men suspect your tale to be untrue,
Keep probability—some say—in view.
. . . Assemble, first, all casual bits and scraps
That may shake down into a world perhaps;
. . . Let the erratic course they steer surprise
Their own, and your own and your readers' eyes;
—ROBERT GRAVES, *The Devil's Advice to Story-tellers*

Leaving our wives, companions, and children behind to cope with Washington living (we had rented a row house on 5th and Peabody Street, next door to a high school principal and his wife who promised to look after Joy and eighteen-month old Laurie), we departed for special training at a secret site. The location of the site was no secret to our wives, who were able to easily pinpoint the location by interrogating their husbands about the length of time of the bus ride, the local climate, topography, and so forth. And although the training site was secret in the beginning, stories later appeared in the press alluded to the CIA training site in southeastern Virginia.

After a three-hour bus ride, "WARNING: U.S. GOVERNMENT PROPERTY" signs began to appear. A mile or so later we turned in at a gate and were waved through by security guards. After a twenty-minute ride winding through a pine forest, the bus emerged in front of a quadrangle of barracks: The Farm.

Thumping a swagger stick, a leather-faced figure stood by the bus as we got off. He immediately barked at us to line up and stand at attention. Once we had formed up to his satisfaction, the gravel-throated officer walked back and forth in front of us, stopped, and spoke.

"Welcome to The Farm. My name is Hodacil. I will be your supervisor, disciplinarian, and chaplain. You are here for six months. Reveille is at six. Physical training at six thirty, followed by a three-mile run. After breakfast, you begin your training in 'candlesteen' warfare with courses on weapons, explosives, sabotage, living off the land, silent killing, parachute jumping.

"After six months, you will undergo a three-week comprehensive field exercise when you will live off the land and put in practice those 'candelsteen' techniques. After the 'COMP' is over, you will return to D.C.

"One last thing. You can quit any time. But while you're here, you will do what I tell you, when I tell you. Don't smart-ass me, and remember, you can't shit an old shitter!"

For the next six months we remembered.

—◊◊◊—

I wondered if I had gotten on the right bus. Silent killing? Sabotage? I had thought this special training was going to be about recruiting agents in Viennese Rathskellers and pilfering secrets in Istanbul souks. I looked around at our group. One or two could be smoke jumpers or linebackers, but most were nondescript school teachers, bank clerks, or management trainees. None looked like potential saboteurs or silent killers.

I had no time to reflect, however. Hodacil was barking for us to double-time over to the mess hall.

Bert

My eyelids were still crusted when Hodacil rousted us out the next morning for physical training. Bert, the instructor, looked like Charles Atlas in the ad about "making MEN out of ninety-eight-pound weaklings!" He was bald and barrel-chested. His neck was so thick it was hard to tell where it ended and his shoulders began, and his top-heavy torso obscured the wiry muscled legs that pumped up and down while he led our exercises.

Bert had been a Presbyterian minister and lived by the credo that the human body was a gift from God and abusing or neglecting it was a sin. His physical prowess was legend at The Farm, where he dove through ice-crusted ponds to retrieve ducks shot by fellow instructors and dropped them at their feet like a faithful Labrador.

I was a disappointment to Bert. I made it through the push-ups and duck-walks and wheezed along the three-mile run. But I failed him on the obstacle course, a satanic steeplechase of greased poles to shimmy up, ravines, and three walls. The ten-foot wall was my nemesis.

I could vault over the six-foot wall, pull myself up and over the eight-foot wall, but the ten-foot wall stymied me. Others danced up the barrier like Jimmy Cagney in *Yankee Doodle Dandy*, but I always bounced off and landed on my back as the rest of the group ran by, splattering mud on their prostrate classmate.

The forays against the ten-foot wall took a toll on my rib cage, and I began sneaking around the wall when Bert wasn't looking. One day, however, Bert caught me as I was making my furtive detour. He had a pained look on his face and called me over to where he was standing. "St. Martin," he said. "one day you will find yourself in a gulag behind a wall like that one. If you can't make it over, you will spend the rest of your life in a Siberian stalag. Now get back there and try again. And again. And again, until you make it over that wall."

I wanted to tell Bert about my battered rib cage, but he would have just told me to "work it out," so I went back to try again. I crouched down, dug in my toes, and ran toward the wall. My momentum almost carried me over, but as I grabbed for the top, I slipped and fell, hitting the ground hard. The wind was knocked out of me, and my eyes began to water, and I could just make out Bert standing there, unmoved.

His stone-faced look angered me, probably as Bert intended. I picked myself up and went back for another try. Pawing dirt and snorting, I took a deep breath and ran. I hit the wall so hard I was carried straight up, and suddenly I found myself on top. I swung my leg over and, for a moment, just sat there savoring my triumph. Then I dropped down on the other side, where Bert stood waiting, a trace of a smile on the ex-pastor's face. We jogged together the rest of the way, and at the end of the course Bert pressed a piece of paper in my hand, a poem he had copied by hand:

It's the plugging away that will win you the day
So don't be a piker old pard:
Just draw on your grit, it's easy to quit,
It's the keeping the chin up that's hard!

I ran into Bert ten years later on another obstacle course called Vietnam, where "keeping the chin up was hard."

The formal course began with weapons training, learning how to assemble, disassemble, and fire Russian Kalashnikovs, Israeli Uzis, American violin-case Thompson submachine guns, and "Swedish Ks."

I was told that covert merchants had fanned out during the Cold War, buying up weapons of foreign origin, including a large number of Swedish K submachine guns. A number of these "sterile" weapons were allegedly stored behind the Iron Curtain and later reportedly unearthed by KGB canines. Some remain buried to confound future archaeologists.

Lanavoski (Ski) taught us the "art of silent killing." To Ski the jewel of the crown was the stiletto, which, when inserted into the jugular, would dispatch the victim without a gurgle. One volunteer for Ski's stiletto demonstration still bears a four-pointed scar on his neck as a reminder of Ski's "jewel."

The Survival Course was a welcome change. We spent two weeks in the field learning carving fishhooks, setting snares, and cooking three-star bouillabaisses of grub worms.

Suturing

Holmes had more than once left the classroom when a live rabbit was to be chloroformed beseeching his demonstrator not to let it squeak.
—MATTHEW PEARL, *The Dante Club*

The course on first aid began with a slide show depicting ripped abdomens, severed limbs, and distended intestines. When the lights came on at the end of the slide show, two instructors were standing on either side of a stainless steel operating table holding down a live rabbit.

We sat transfixed like premed students at their first postmortem. One instructor held up a bottle of chloroform, sprinkled a few drops on a wad of cotton, and put the wad over the rabbit's nose. When the rabbit stopped twitching, the instructor held up a scalpel for our inspection and then made an incision along the rabbit's stomach, leaving a thin red trickle to mark the scalpel's route.

The instructor then held up a needle and began to sew up the rabbit, pausing to identify the "I," "H," and "T" stitches. He completed the operation with the "X" tie-off stitch and held up the sutured comatose rabbit up for our inspection. He seemed disappointed we didn't applaud.

Several minutes later the rabbit stumbled off the table and groggily hopped out the door. That was when we applauded.

No one had noticed that a member of our class had slipped out the back when the stitching operation began. Cauley didn't return until the operation was over, and the instructor was announcing that the class would be divided into two-man teams for a live suturing exercise the following day.

Cauley

Cauley was a study in perpetual motion. A feisty redhead, he was unable to sit still, continually slapping his knees and cracking his knuckles and coming out with Gaelic aphorisms only he understood. In the field Cauley was the class leprechaun, somersaulting down trails, darting out from behind trees, and playing Puck's bad boy.

The evening following the suture demonstration, we were sitting around the bar in the recreation room when Cauley burst in, jumped up on one of the bar stools, and called for silence. "Tonight the bells of freedom are ringing out over The Farm!" he said. "This Irish mother's son has just liberated all those pink-eyed prisoners on death row! No scalpel will cut into their pink tummies, because at this very minute they are hopping down the freedom bunny trail!"

Cauley's outbursts were usually ignored, but this time he had our full attention. He told us how he had broken into the lab where the rabbits were kept, opened all their cages, and sent them hopping off into the woods.

Cauley the clown had now become the "great rabbit liberator"!

When the empty cages were discovered, neither the training staff nor Hodacil were amused. An extra mile was added to our morning run, but we didn't mind, because Hodacil had to run with us to make sure we went the distance.

The Air Drop

Using powdered lime, we had marked out the "T" on an open field selected as the drop zone (DZ). When the plane appeared overhead, we threw out a smoke grenade to indicate the wind direction and that the DZ was secure. We had been ordered to remain concealed off the field until the drop was over and the plane dropped down to "buzz" the DZ.

The airdrop almost went as planned. The plane made several passes, parachuting bundles rumored to contain beer and cigarettes. Instead of waiting for the signal that the drop was over, the impatient Cauley rushed out onto the DZ and began tearing at the straps of the nearest bundle. Concentrating on untangling the straps, Cauley didn't hear the plane coming in over the trees to buzz the DZ. It was heading straight for Cauley.

We shouted warnings to Cauley, who couldn't hear over the noise of the plane's engines. When he finally did look up and saw that the plane heading directly at him, he froze. Then he panicked and apparently lost his bearings, because he suddenly began running down the field in the same direction as the plane. We watched in disbelief as our "Charlie Chaplin" churned down the DZ, the plane almost nipping at his heels. Cauley and the plane reached the end of the DZ at almost the same time. The plane pulled up sharply over the trees, but the downdraft from the engines sucked Cauley up into the air and then dropped him unceremoniously back onto the DZ. Yesterday's rabbit liberator lay spread-eagled in the mud as his classmates rushed out to retrieve the spoils.

Out the Door

I didn't look forward to parachute training. Defying gravity with a flimsy nylon canopy was risky at best, and Hodacil's jokes about "streamers" and ripped crotches and his song about "blood upon his risers and blood upon his chute, his intestines were a hangin' from his paratrooper's boot," didn't help.

Hodacil was a seasoned paratrooper, however, and an excellent trainer and in two weeks had turned us into mindless jump-happy automatons, standing up, hooking up, and jumping out the door with only slight pushes.

We made five jumps. I preferred the night jumps, because I couldn't see the ground coming up at me. After our last jump, Hodacil pinned on our parachute wings, then took them back the next day "for security reasons."

The Comp

The finale to our training was The Comp (comprehensive field exercise), the field test putting into practice what we had or had not learned over the past six months.

The day before it began, we were issued French identity cards and told to stand by. At midnight two trucks drove up to the barracks, disgorging hooded figures shouting French epithets: *Emmerdeurs!* Shitheads. *Cochons!* Pigs. Prodding us with bayonets, they herded us into trucks. After an hour's jarring ride scraping trees and slipping in and out of ruts, we pulled up in front of Stalag 13.

Searchlights swept along the ten-foot-high fence around the stalag. Triple strands of barbed wire were strung along the top. Sentinels with guard dogs patrolled the perimeter.

We were shoved through the gate into the stockade and marched off to be interrogated. The interrogators handed us confessions to sign, but since heroics come easy in make-believe, we all refused. We were then hauled outside and put in "the hole." Hunger and the chill of a long cold night broke our resistance, and we all signed confessions.

We were split up into four-man teams. Team Fox—*Equipe Renard*—consisted of Jean Gabin, Jacques Pipi, Con Rouge, and Jules Salaud, myself. We were locked in a cell, where we stayed until nightfall, when a figure darted by our cell and tossed a packet through the bars. The packet was our escape kit and contained a compass, canine repellent, and a map marked with the coordinates of the rendez-vous point where we were to wait to be contacted by the "Resistance."

I almost botched the escape. Con Rouge left first, breaking out of the cell and spraying canine repellent along the bottom of the fence before climbing over, followed by Pipi and Jean Gabin. Dropping down on the other side, the three crouched in the woods waiting for me to join them. When I got to the fence, I threw my poncho up on top to protect me when I climbed over the barbed wire. I threw too hard, however, and the poncho went over the fence, dropping on the other side. When I climbed up the fence and swung a leg over, my pant leg ripped, and I suddenly found myself pilloried like a scarecrow. Cold air rushed through my crotch as the others yelled at me to hurry.

I tugged frantically at my pant leg until it finally tore off, and I swung over and dropped down on the other side just as the searchlight beam came to a stop on my pant leg, fluttering in the wind like a tattered pennant. We could hear laughter drifting out of the stalag. Bert was probably sitting there smiling.

We arrived at the rendezvous point and made camp under a fallen tree. The next morning we thatched our lean-to, set snares, baited fish lines, and waited to be contacted.

For five days while we waited, we went out only long enough to inspect our snares and fishhooks. The rain didn't let up, and we spent most of the time sitting inside the lean-to watching the fire. Our snares remained empty, our fishhooks denuded. On the fifth day we heard noises coming from the back of the lean-to, and we thought a bear had gotten at our rations. We had been issued emergency rations with the warning that breaking into them for anything other than a real emergency, was cause for a failing grade in survival training.

When we peered back into the back of the lean-to, two wide eyes belonging to "Pipi" Cauley peered back. He was biting into a chocolate bar from his rations, and when he saw us staring at him, he growled that he was starving and "sick of this Mahatma Gandhi routine." He added that that he couldn't care less if he got an "F" in survival. Without comment, we turned around and went back to watching the fire.

While we had been preoccupied with Cauley, someone had dropped an oil-skin packet in front of the lean-to. It contained directions to a cached rubber boat and signal codes for contacting the submarine standing by offshore.

We broke camp and were putting out the fire when Con Rouge, who had gone for a final check of the snares, came back with a partridge. We toasted it over the coals and ate it in front of the sulking Cauley.

We located the rubber boat cached under a log and at midnight signaled the submarine. When the all clear was flashed we paddled out to the "submarine," a rusting fishing trawler fitted out with a stovepipe periscope. The captain invited us on board for coffee and donuts and handed us a new set of orders that instructed us to proceed to the village of L'Espion and contact the Resistance leader at the Le Chat Noir Café.

The main street of L'Espion was lined on either side with plywood mock-ups of la patisserie, la boulangerie, le Hotel de Ville, and Le Chat Noir—the bakery, butcher shop, town hall, and the Black Cat Café.

Candles flickered on red-checked tablecloths inside the Chat Noir. As we entered, we noticed Monsieur Moulin (Hodacil) sitting at the far table. Gabin walked over to the table and introduced himself as the "foie gras salesman." Hodacil's reply that foie gras was for fat "bourgeois-zees." Our bona fides established, he invited to sit down to join him in a glass of wine.

Hodacil toasted Les Reynards, slid an envelope across the table containing our missions for the next month, and got up. He wished us Bon Chance and said the wine was "on the house."

We read over our assigned missions, finished the wine, and went out to pick up supplies behind La Boulangerie. The Team Fox duffle bag contained four Swedish Ks and ammunition, several packets of C-3 plastic explosive along with fuses, detonating cords, and time pencils. We buried the duffel bag, divided up the weapons and supplies, and headed back into the woods.

For the next four weeks we covered an area bigger than most state parks, blowing bridges, ambushing enemy patrols, mining roads, and derailing trains. Blowing up the fuel dump, however, almost spelled finis to Team Fox.

The dump consisted of ten oil drums lashed together behind a wire fence. We cut through the fence and taped a shape charge of C3 explosive onto one of the drums. We set the time pencil for thirty seconds, giving us enough time to get away before the charge blew.

Time pencils, like fever thermometers, are delicate instruments and not always reliable. Whether it was human error or a defective time pencil that set the charge off prematurely, we never knew. We were on our way out through the fence when the charge exploded, knocking us all to the ground and sending a geyser of crankcase oil fifty feet into the air. The black oil raining down from the geyser soaked our fatigues and left us smelling like the crew from the *Amoco Cadiz* tanker that ran aground off Alaska.

When we walked into L'Espion for the final exercise, the teams already there made a point of holding their noses when we passed.

The last week of the Comp in L'Espion was a simulated run-up to the D-day landings. Teams stumbled over each other trying to recruit agents in the Chat Noir, putting sugar in the gas tanks of SS armored cars, and cranking out leaflets. Radio antennas that sprouted around the town were pointed toward London, waiting for the "dit-dit-dit-dah" of Beethoven's Fifth to signal that the landings were under way.

When the "V" signal came over the air, we ran out tossing cherry bombs, firing Swedish Ks in the air, and marching out to welcome the "liberators" in the form of

Hodacil parachuting in for a stand-up landing with a bottle of champagne. When he popped the cork, it was the signal that The Comp was over.

Two days later we became the first class to graduate from The Farm. A Headquarters VIP delivered the commencement address and told us we were now members of the Agency's elite. Just how "elite" we would find out when we got back to Washington.

Hodacil came by the day we left. He said he had mixed feelings—joy and jubilation—about our leaving and presented a rabbit's foot to Cauley. He said that he would sleep better knowing we were out there "stemming the tide of red aggression." The old shitter to the end. The flashbacks for that first class are still fresh, the paramilitary catechisms, the suturing and stilettos, living off the land, the moonlight parachute jumps, and the campfire comraderie.

The curriculum, however, was an anomaly. We were immersed in a World War II resistance culture, which had long since given way to doctrines of Che Guevarra and Mao Zedong. Although we were never called on to garrote a Nazi sentinel or blow up the guns of Navarone, the fundamentals still applied whether winning hearts and minds in Southeast Asia or tunneling under East Berlin.

Most enduring were the ties that bound us. When meeting later, eating sticky rice along the Mekong, drinking Singapore Slings at Raffles, or watching pirogues paddling up the Congo, we would hark back to liberated rabbits, "stiletto" Ski, and the "old shitter."

As I write, Jean Gabin and I are the only members of Team Fox still alive. Jacques Pipi and Con Rouge "bought the farm," and their names are inscribed on the rotunda wall.

CHAPTER 3: **The Flap**

For nothing is secret, that shall not be made manifest; neither anything hid, that shall not be known and come abroad.

—*Gospel of Luke*

J building, along with I, K, and L, was once located behind the trees lining the Lincoln Memorial reflecting pool. The temporary prefabs served as temporary government offices during World War II but for some reason had been bypassed by postwar demolition crews.

J building's frame was reverberating from couriers pounding along the warped linoleum corridors, delivering "OPERATIONAL IMMEDIATE" and "FLASH" messages. Branch chiefs and desk officers nervously awaited their summons from the deputy director of operations. A flap was in the air.

"Flap" is a semantic holdover from the days of steaming open flaps of envelopes to "read other peoples mail." It currently refers to a "blown" or "compromised" activity, an operational meltdown.

The epicenter of the flap rocking J building was Kaltenborn, a small town in Bavaria. A displaced persons (DP) camp had been taken over to serve as a training site for political action cadre. The townspeople jokingly referred to the site as Wienerschnitzel.

The political action trainees were mostly from East Germany, and after their training in Kaltenborn, they were reinfiltrated into their home country either to sow the seeds of counterrevolution or to go underground as "sleepers" and wait for the anticipated uprising. Kaltenborn citizens joked about Wienerschnitzel but didn't really worry about the strange goings-on in the camp, because local merchants were Wienerschnitzel's primary suppliers.

One day, however, a reporter passing through Kaltenborn heard talk about a "secret" installation outside of town and decided to investigate. He drove out past the camp, parked his jeep, and climbed a knoll overlooking the camp. His camera was equipped with a long-range lens, and he took photographs of the DPs mixing Molotov cocktails, printing leaflets, and engaging in hand-to-hand combat.

His photographs appeared a week later on the front page of a Frankfurt news-paper under the caption "CIA cooks Wienerschnitzel in Kaltenborn."

The exposé was officially denounced by the German government as a "KGB fabrication." Privately, the German chancellor was furious and called the U.S. high commissioner on the carpet to complain about the flap and the embarrassment it had caused. The high commissioner ordered the Station to shut down the operation immediately, and in less than a week, more than a hundred CIA case officer trainers were on their way back to Headquarters.

The ignominious return of these officers to Headquarters coincided unfortunately with our return from The Farm. The dual influx from Germany and The Farm led the deputy director of operations to issue a directive putting a temporary "hold" on further overseas assignments.

The recent graduates from the Farm were sent to "the pool" to wait for the dust to settle.

The Pool

The pool is a way station, a dumping ground for the unassigned. Our group spent most of the day in the cafeteria drinking coffee, grousing about our "limbo" status, and sitting around waiting to be called.

We were occasionally given odd jobs in Registry, sorting and filing the backlog of documents yellowing with age in an Arlington warehouse. Going through these old documents reminded me of rummaging through old family letters in an attic trunk. These letters, however, were dispatches from overseas Stations, and we read the best of them out loud, vicariously transporting ourselves to locales such as Hong Kong, Calcutta, or Montevideo, where we hoped one day to be assigned.

Some of the dispatches read like pulp fiction, with passages describing agent concubines nibbling the ears of Middle East potentates, chauffeurs blackmailing Balkan ambassadors, double agents being "tripled" and then sent back to their Soviet KGB handlers. While the dispatches made good reading, they reminded us of an operational world of which it seemed we would never be a part. Two months had passed, and we were still treading water in the pool, unassigned.

Three members of our group tired of waiting and signed on as polygraph operator trainees. The rest of us decided to strike out on our own and approach the country desks directly.

Trading on my rubber company experience, I arranged an interview with a Southeast Asia personnel officer. The interviewer seemed impressed with my background in the rubber company and told me he thought there was an opening coming up soon. He was going to tell me more when something in my file caught his attention. He quickly closed the file and told me he had been mistaken. The opening had already been filled.

Back in the cafeteria, when I mentioned the aborted interview, two others in our group described similar experiences of abruptly aborted interviews terminated for no apparent reason. Our conclusion was that there must be something in our files, some common denominator that was responsible for these curt dismissals.

It was Jean Gabin who discovered the common denominator. He was being interviewed when the interviewer was called away. Gabin immediately reached across the desk, took the file, and began reading through it. Inside were records of physical exams, polygraph tests, training evaluations, and various administrative papers. He found nothing out of the ordinary until he came to the end. On the last page two large letters were stamped in red in the middle: "PM."

We eventually found out from a friendly secretary that the letters stood for "paramilitary." This was the "elite" group the commencement speaker had referred to.

PM

The Operations Directorate was caste layered. The top layer is made up of the brahmins, the foreign intelligence (FI) officers. Real spies. The next layer is composed of the sudras, the political action/psychological warfare (PP) officers. The bottom layer consists of the untouchables, paramilitary (PM) officers.

The letters PM, like Hester Prynne's "A" in Hawthorne's *Scarlet Letter*, branded us as outcasts. PM officers were excluded from the "better" locales like Paris and Vienna, where the aperitif and savoir-faire are de riguer and the stiletto and plastic explosives are frowned upon. FI and PP officers looked down on PM officers as the bulls in the Agency's china shop.

Now that we knew our place, we also knew where to look for assignments. It was rumored there were openings in certain Asian and African locations for PM officers. I decided to try for Bushido.

Bushido, steeped in a culture of the tea ceremony, flower arranging, and classic Noh and Kabuki theater, was an unlikely venue for paramilitary operations, but the fledgling government for the most part turned a blind eye on the activities of its former enemy.

I applied for an assignment to Bushido and was accepted. A month later I left "the pool" behind and boarded a Pan American flight for Edo, the capital of Bushido.

PART II
Operations

I think it may very reasonably be required
of every writer that he keeps within the bounds of
possibility, and still remembers that what it is not possible for man to perform, it is scarce possible for man
to believe he did perform.

—HENRY FIELDING, *Tom Jones*

INTRODUCTION

—ᗰ—

I n 1947 President Harry Truman, fed up with tea leaf readers and rumor peddlers knocking at the back door of the White House, established a national
marketplace for information, the Central Intelligence Agency. To direct this
new agency, he chose Allen Dulles, a pipe-smoking savant, who had served with
the World War II spy organization, the Office of Strategic Services (OSS). To staff
the organization, the new director first brought in professors, researchers, and
scholars and grouped them into the Directorate of Intelligence (DI).

To balance this intellectual ivory tower, Dulles sent out a call to former OSS
cloak-and-dagger colleagues. These he grouped into the Directorate of Operations
(DO) and cached them in "temporary" buildings behind the reflecting pool of the
Lincoln Memorial.

The Directorate of Operations took pride in its lack of structure. Its organization chart was a maze of zigzag broken lines and convoluted circles, not
unlike the circles Dante passes through in the Divine Comedy during his journey
through purgatory.

Entering the first circle, a candidate for covert service first had to pass physical and psychological examinations and the lie detector test. If the candidate
passed these tests, he or she would enter the second circle where the candidate
would be trained in the clandestine arts and science. When the tradecraft training was successfully completed, the candidate could enter into the third and final
circle, operations.

The operations circle was a carnavalian merry-go-round, where informants
and agents were recruited and later "doubled"; cabals were hatched and aborted;
governments propped up and toppled; desert chieftains "godfathered" and left
dangling from lamp posts; ballerina troupes sent off on world tours to vanish in
the mist; hill tribes formed into guerrilla battalions and later abandoned. I entered
the third circle in Bushido.

CHAPTER 4: **Bushido**

The empire of Bushido, founded eight hundred years before Columbus discovered America, was steeped in tradition, customs, and well-defined codes of conduct. Pried open to the West in the mid-nineteenth century, Bushido came on stage as a world power when it defeated the Russians at the turn of the twentieth century and continued to play a dominant role in East Asia until the mid-1940s, when war ravaged the country. The country was only beginning to recover when I arrived after a twenty-four-hour flight on a Pan American "clipper." My family, increased by one with the birth of our son, Kent, in Washington, D.C., would follow later by boat on the American President Lines.

I was met and taken by jeep to the air base where our installation was located. Although it was a large air base, our installation was easy to spot in the base's farthest corner. It consisted of a long green windowless Quonset hut and a large hangar. The sign at the gate to the site read, "RESTRICTED AREA: RESEARCH IN PROGRESS."

When I entered the green building, even though it was nine o'clock in the morning, several Steve Canyon look-alikes in baggy flight suits, former Flying Tiger pilots, were drinking beer at the rattan bar near the entrance. I walked to the far end of the building, where the chief's office was located and where I could hear a loud voice shouting on the telephone. Waiting until the shouting stopped, I knocked and was told to come in. Colonel Applewhite was smoking a cigar and motioned me to a chair while he continued talking on the phone. After he hung up, he walked over, shook my hand, and then motioned me to a rattan chair opposite his desk.

"Welcome to Bushido. Great place, but am afraid you've come at a bad time. We're in the middle of a big flap! Two case officers were shot down over China yesterday, including the one you were supposed to replace. All overflight operations have been canceled, and your slot has been eliminated."

The smoke from Applewhite's cigar fortunately obscured the dumbfounded look on my face. Overflight operations? I recalled the personnel officer having been vague about my assignment, saying I would be "filled in" when I got to Bushido. As Applewhite contemplated the smoke rings from his cigar coiling up toward the ceiling, I tried to absorb what he had just told me. Another flap. The rain cloud, like the one perpetually hanging over Mister Magoo, had apparently followed me across the Pacific!

As the cigar smoke lifted, I saw Applewhite looking at me. He must have known what I was thinking, and he did his best to cheer me up.

"Don't worry, son," he said. "I'm not going to send you back to Headquarters. We've had flaps before, and we'll find something to keep you busy until another slot opens up, although I can't tell you when that will be."

Just then a communications officer knocked and came in and handed the base chief a cable, and said, "Another FLASH from panic city wanting to know who authorized American case officers on mainland overflights."

As the base chief grabbed the cable, I decided it was a good time to leave, before he changed his mind about sending me back to Headquarters. I slipped out the door and walked toward the bar at the end of the hall to mull over my latest misfortune.

My slot had been eliminated and two case officers had been shot down over China. I knew, however, that I shouldn't feel sorry for myself. If I had arrived earlier, it might have been me hunkering down in a bamboo cage somewhere in Red China. In fact, as it turned out, the two case officers spent twenty-two years as prisoners of the Red Chinese before, as a "goodwill gesture" during President Richard Nixon's historic visit to China, they were released.

Ming

A most solemn graveyard ditty, the mutual consolations of suicide lovers remembering the pangs and the delights of supernal love in the infernal groves.

—HENRY THOREAU, *Walden*

The first priority was cleaning up the detritus from the flap. Safe houses, where agents lived while being trained, were turned back to their landlords and quit claims paid. Agents in training were paid off and terminated, with most of them melting into Edo's Chinatown.

Most of them, but not all.

Ming had been a promising agent. According to his case officer, he was intelligent and highly motivated and was eager to return to his homeland and join the "counterrevolution." Since he was a Mandarin, Ming got preferential treatment, including his own safe house with a live-in Chinese maid.

Ming was a good student. He asked questions, took notes, and studied hard, at least in the beginning. Later, during his training, however, his case officer noticed Ming's concentration flagging and initial enthusiasm beginning to wane. He became nervous and irritable and seemed to have difficulty concentrating. His case officer attributed the change to Ming realizing that his training was coming to an end and that he would soon have to forgo the comfort and security of his safe house for a dangerous future in his former homeland.

Ming also began taking more frequent and longer tea breaks during his training sessions, disappearing into the kitchen, where he could be overheard having whispered conversations with the maid. His case officer found it strange that a member of the Mandarin class would spend so much time in conversation with a servant but attributed the tête-à-têtes to Ming's loneliness and desire to talk to someone in his native language.

A week before Ming was to finish his training, his case officer arrived at the safe house and found no sign of either Ming or the maid. Both of them had apparently disappeared. Several days later John Madison, the security officer, got a phone call from his Bushidan liaison contact, Lieutenant Basho. Basho advised Madison that two bodies, in what was apparently a double suicide, had been discovered in a bamboo grove not far from the air base. One body was a Chinese female with papers indicating she was employed at the air base. Her family had been notified and had taken the body back to her native village. The other body was an unidentified Chinese male, and Basho asked Madison to come down to the police station and possibly identify the body as a base "employee."

Basho had been helpful in the past in dealing with agents who slipped away from the training site and ran up bills in the tea houses and brothels, bills they couldn't pay because they had no money. Madison would come and pick up these "strays," pay their bills, and bring them back to their safe houses. It was an arrangement that suited Basho fine, because it relieved him of having to make out long reports that in the end would only upset his superiors.

Madison asked Sammy Lee, a Chinese-American case officer, to accompany him to the Station. When they arrived, Basho led them down to the basement, where the body had been laid out on a wooden table.

Basho went over and pulled back the sheet. Lee immediately cried out, "Ming, my beloved nephew!"

Lee's outburst was followed by effusive sobbing. Basho, probably aware that the crocodile tears were for his benefit, looked on sympathetically, visibly relieved that the avuncular Mr. Lee would take the corpse off his hands. Once Lee's tears had subsided, Basho told Madison Mr. Lee was free to take his nephew's body away so he could make arrangements for his final ancestral journey. Madison and Lee carried Ming out to the back of the police station where the jeep was parked. Rigor mortis made it difficult to wedge the body into the back of the jeep, but the two men finally succeeded and propped Ming up on the rear seat. They wrapped a blanket around him, leaving only his two unblinking eyes peering out into the darkness.

When they arrived at the air base, the guard shined his flashlight into the jeep. Madison explained that his friend in the back had drunk "too much sake," but the guard decided to look for himself. When he got closer, however, he recoiled from the odor emanating from Ming and waved the jeep through. They drove to the special hangar and laid Ming's body on a stretcher in the far corner until arrangements could be made for his disposition.

I was told the following day to report at midnight to the hangar to assist in a special operation. Ming had been zipped into a plastic body bag, and I helped Madison and another officer strap on "life belts," in which lead weights had been inserted in place of Styrofoam packets.

An hour later, Bing Aldren and his crew, the Steve Canyons I had seen at the bar when I first arrived, drove up in a jeep looking bleary eyed and hung over. We followed the captain and crew into the plane and laid Ming's body on a canvas tarpaulin. When the cargo door slammed shut, the odor of Ming's formaldehyde and the crew's alcohol combined to leave the plane smelling like a cross between a drunk tank and a morgue.

The plane taxied down the runway, yawing from side to side, sparks flying as the wingtips scraped the tarmac until it finally lifted off. Once the plane had leveled off, Algren's voice came over the loudspeaker. "Twenty minutes to Edo Bay Memorial Cemetery. Prepare for burial at sea!"

Fifteen minutes later, the yellow warning light began blinking. We unhinged the door, and a welcome blast of cold air suddenly emptied the plane of the fumes that had almost overpowered us since takeoff. Sparks from the engine flashed by as we pushed Ming's body until his feet stuck out in the slipstream. When the green light flashed, we gave Ming a final shove just as the plane banked sharply, sending him and his pallbearers crashing against the plane's metal rib cage on the other side of the plane.

Algren's voice came over the speaker. "Sorry about that. Unexpected turbulence. We'll go around again for another pass."

The green light flashed again, and we gave Ming another shove. We could see the foamy whitecaps on the black swells of the sea, but again the plane banked sharply to the left. This time we grabbed onto the cargo rings to keep from crashing back onto the fuselage, but one of the straps of the body bag got caught on a cargo ring, leaving him dangling halfway out the door, his body buffeted like a rag doll in the slipstream.

We decided not to wait for Algren to make another pass, crawled over to Ming, and cut the strap to his shroud, while at the same time giving him a final shove. Ming's body, like a ghostly apparition, levitated upright for a moment and then dropped out of sight. We crawled over to the door and peered out to see Ming's body dropping end over end until it finally splashed into the bay. We then threw out the sprigs of cherry blossoms his "uncle" had asked us to scatter over his grave.

Requiescat in pace.

PM Librarian

In the weeks that followed, I was given odd jobs such as stuffing balloons with leaflets. Unpredictable wind currents blew most of the leaflets back over Edo to the delight of its citizenry, who were badly in need of toilet paper.

I was still unassigned, so when there was an opening for an assistant librarian, I swallowed my paramilitary pride and took it.

The position of librarian was a sinecure for the widow of a base case officer who died after eating a poisoned fugu (blowfish). Ruth drowned her grief with gin and tonics and rarely showed up in the library. She was happy, however, to learn she would have an assistant so she could devote more time to her Beefeaters.

The library consisted of a *Webster's Dictionary*, a set of *World Book Encyclopedias*, Erick Ambler's *Epitaph for a Spy*, James Michener's *Sayonara*, and a biography of Richard Sorge, the famous Russian spy who operated in East Asia during World War II. I persuaded Ruth to authorize me to buy more books to fill the library shelves.

I scoured the numerous kiosks of Edo's Seiki district, which were lined with book kiosks displaying woodblock erotica, cardboard color comics of *The Legend of Momotaro the Peach Boy* and *The Tale of the Genji*, and English-language hard covers and paperbacks. I also purchased an album of erotic woodprints. The library shelves were almost full when the first case officers came in to browse.

I persuaded several case officers to take advantage of the library's newly created Intelligence Coordination Section (ICS). Research was the word I hoped would attract case officers, who found research dull and onerous at worst and a distasteful distraction at best. I figured that if I could provide them with background pieces to fill out and enliven their dispatches, they would be grateful and I would gain access to that operations fraternity from which I was still excluded.

My first client was a case officer who wanted background material on the Sons of Samurai, a little-known fledgling ultranationalist organization. I sifted through embassy telegrams, newspaper clippings, and magazine articles and put together enough material for a report, adding footnotes from the Edo Warrior's Code and the Samurai Code of Conduct. I signed the report, "Deputy Director, Intelligence Research Section (IRS)," a title of my own invention.

The case officer must have liked the report, because I became inundated with requests from other case officers for research papers. And when the next Table of Organization appeared, there was a box for the Intelligence Coordination Section with dotted lines leading to the Operations Sections. My nose was under the operational tent.

Several months later, the Sons of Samurai case officer alerted me to an opening in the Political Action Section. I applied and was accepted. I turned in my badge as deputy librarian for that of a junior case officer.

Case Officer

Man is too addicted to the intoxicating mixture of adolescent bucca-neering and adult perfidy to relinquish it entirely.

—P. D. JAMES, *The Children of Men*

The case officer is the Agency's foot soldier. His primary role is recruiting and handling agents, who range from chambermaids to cabinet ministers, office clerks to tribal chiefs.

Case officers, covert professionals, should not be confused with caseworkers. The latter are overt professionals who can openly take pride in their profession. Case officers have to remain anonymous and cannot publicly declare their profession except to other case officers. Society has no respectable niche for the spy. His profession is regarded at best as sinister, at worst as ignoble.

Case officers and caseworkers do, however, have one thing in common: unusual clientele. Their "cases" range from unsavory, paranoid, and congenital liars to renegades and patriots, each requiring special handling.

The Agency case officer fits no standard profile. He can be Peter Pan, Peck's bad boy, Walter Mitty, or John Smiley. He plays a variety of roles, depending on his target: the anticommunist evangelist excoriating the "Red Satan," a Fagin trainer of thieves, or a recruiter of scavengers to pick through nuclear trash bins.

The case officer blends in with his surroundings and, like the chameleon, can change covers quickly. His tasks range from sticking pins in Khaddafi dolls, slipping aphrodisiacs to unsuspecting Soviets, or persuading foreign leaders to take a lie detector test.

Case officers are expendable. If a case officer is "burned," the Agency will deny him, although it may later reinstate him after a cooling off period in Registry's catacombs. The case officer can also be fired, or terminated, with or without "prejudice."

As a junior case officer, I reported to George, a senior case officer who spoke fluent Bushidan. He liked to sprinkle his guidance and directions to his junior case officers with Bushidan proverbs. He wasn't a good recruiter, because he found it difficult to bring himself to corrupt the "pure Bushidan soul."

George was chief of the Political Operations Section, but he didn't have anyone to cover the Bushidan labor organizations leading the charge against the presence of American military bases in Bushido. He directed me to cover the Bushidan labor movement.

George gave me a series of tasks. First, study the Bushidan labor movement. Second, establish contacts and elicit information. Third, recruit an agent in the labor field. This was the sum of my direction and guidance. No manuals to follow, no case studies to read over. There was one primary rule of engagement: don't get caught.

The headquarters of Carbo, the coal miners union, at #75 Hirotsuki-cho, was hard to find. Address numbers are in order of their construction date, #1 possibly a hundred yards from #2 if a number of other shops had been built in between. Since I didn't know the chronology of the buildings on Hirotsuki-cho, I stopped at the nearest fire station for directions. Most of the firemen were outside climbing up their ladders to practice juggling acts for the coming cherry blossom festival, but I finally found one who wasn't busy and who escorted me to #75.

Carbo headquarters was in an old warehouse with a large red and white banner over the door. I knocked, didn't get an answer, and knocked again. Finally, I pushed the door open, went inside, and found myself standing in front of fifty or sixty Bushidans wearing red headbands. They were all sitting cross-legged, busily painting placards, probably for the next anti-American demonstration. When I came in, they looked up, stopped painting, and stared open-mouthed at the foreign intruder. No one moved to welcome me or ask what I wanted. They just stared as if I had dropped in from outer space. I was about to turn around and leave, but since I had come this far, I wasn't going to be put off by their stares and silence. I decided to try to break the ice: "*Ohayo!*" Good morning! "*Gomenasai!*" Excuse me.

No response. They continued squinting and staring at me so I tried again. "*Ohayo, gomenasai!*"

Finally, a few heads turned toward the back to look at one of the sign painters. The painter in question uncrossed his legs, stood up, and walked to where I was standing.

"What you want?" he asked.

I was taken aback by the brusque tone of his question. Bushidans are normally reticent and polite, especially with foreigners. I figured his question sounded brusque because of his limited English. Perhaps if I articulated and spoke slowly, he could understand me better and then interpret for the rest of the group. I began with the cover story I had prepared earlier. "I am writing a book about Bushidan coal miners. I came here because I wanted to learn about coal mining in Bushido and to ask you to arrange a visit to a coal mine where I could talk to miners and their families."

As a cover story, it was short, simple, and direct. I paused to give the spokesman enough time to think and try to interpret what I had said. He hesitated, fingered his headband, and looked around the room. Finally, he began to interpret what I had said. When he paused, I continued my story.

I said I came from a coal-mining region of America (a half-truth, because I lived for three years as a boy in West Virginia) and that my father had been a coal miner who died of black-lung disease (a fiction, because my father had been an army officer).

When I mentioned the black-lung disease, the scourge of miners everywhere, I heard sympathetic sucking "ah-so's" from the audience. The mention of the black-lung disease had apparently broken the ice. I decided it was a good time to stop and bowed to indicate I had finished.

My bow at the end of the story prompted someone to call out for cha-yo: tea. I was led to a long table in the back of the room. I wedged myself in between two sign painters and was served a steaming cup of green tea by a bowing, gold-toothed mama-san in a red and white flowered kimono.

I tried to make small talk with the Bushidans sitting next to me, but their responses were limited to nods, smiles, burps, and sucking noises. When the tea break was over, the hall became quiet. The sign painters were apparently waiting for me to make an "after-tea" speech. I had already exhausted my cover story, so I had to think of another diversion. I thought back to a night in a Shinbaku bar when a group of giggling kimono-clad barmaids tried to teach me the Carbo Buki, the "Coal Miners' Dance." It was simple enough even for an awkward American, a series of "dig-dig," "pick-pick," and "shovel-shovel" motions. I hoped I could remember them.

I got up from the table, stepped back, and bowed to the miners who were still sitting around the extended table. I took out my red bandana handkerchief, folded it into a headband, and tied it around my forehead. I walked over and took a broom that was leaning against the wall and began shuffling around the room making picking and shoveling motions with the broom and scooping up imaginary lumps of coal.

I was beginning to feel foolish dancing solo around the hall with my broom shoveling and picking, and then I heard the sound of clapping. Several sign painters had gotten up and had fallen in behind me, imitating the pick-pick, shovel-shovel motions, and soon I found myself leading a conga line as the rest of the sign painters fell in behind me. I led them around the hall twice and then stopped, bowed, and sat down.

Suddenly, everybody started clapping and a large jug of rice wine was brought to the table. A healthy portion was poured into my cup, and I toasted to "coal miners around the world." After more clapping and toasts to the *gansin*, the foreigner, I was convinced my bona fides had been established. It was a good time to leave.

The spokesman walked with me to the door. When I thanked him for the warm welcome, he replied that I should come back the following week. And "bring suitcase for trip to coal mine."

Owata

When I returned a week later, I was greeted with shouts of *Carbo-bushi-san!* The spokesman introduced me to Kanto, the interpreter who was to accompany me on the trip to the Shiba Owata coal mine in southern Bushido. Kanto, who spoke good English, was the younger brother of the secretary general of Carbo.

The overnight train trip took ten hours. We arrived in Owata as the sun was coming up over the island of Shuku, home to the world's largest undersea coal mine. Its black anthracite veins stretch like tentacles for several miles out under the sea, the veins providing charcoal for hibachis all over Bushido and livelihoods for eight thousand miners.

The Coal Mine

That he should be lowered . . . into those subterranean zones from which no one returns without having their view of life on the surface modified.

—GRAHAM SWIFT, *Ever After*

We were met at the station by Carbo officials, who drove us off in a battered old Studebaker with a Pontiac hood ornament. After paying a courtesy call to the mining company director, we went directly to the mine. I was outfitted with baggy pants, an oil-stained jacket, sloth-toed sandals, and a miner's helmet and headlamp. Kanto and I were then squeezed into bucket-shaped coal cars hooked behind a miniature locomotive.

The train gave several jerks and then clanked off down into the mine. It became pitch black, and it seemed as if the tunnel was closing in around us. Water began dripping on my helmet, and I knew we were out under the sea. We went down past honeycombs of mineshafts braced with wooden posts that creaked and groaned, their echoes reverberating along the tunnels and bouncing off the mine-shafts. We had descended into an underwater mausoleum. The train gave a series of jerks and stopped. When we got out, I could see miners kneeling and lying on their backs, chipping off shards of coal. Figures trotted along the shafts scooping up the shards and then dumping their buckets into the empty coal cars.

Interviewing miners under the sea was not going to be easy, but for my cover story to hold up, I had to try. I duck-waddled along the nearest shaft until I found a niche next to a miner with enough room for me to squat alongside. The miner glanced over his shoulder at his unexpected visitor, nodded, and went back to chipping off shards of coal.

I had been there about ten minutes when he turned and pointed to the empty bucket behind him. If I was going to share his space, I should make myself useful. I nodded and began scooping up shards and dumping them into the coal bucket. I actually welcomed the task, because it took my mind off the cramps and my knotting leg muscles.

I scooped up shards for almost an hour before a bell rang for the lunch break. I leaned back and stretched my legs. The miner offered me one of his rice balls wrapped in seaweed and some of his tea. I thanked him and then asked him about working in the mine, his home and his family. He said he had a wife and four children, liked beer and baseball, and was tired of working in the mine.

Author with Bushido coal miners.

My interview was cut short when the bell rang and we went back to work. The cramps had begun to come back when Kanto came by and said it was time to go. I thanked the miner for sharing his lunch with me. He smiled and nodded, then reached in his pocket and handed me a "souvenir," a black lump of coal sparkling with silver mica chips. My first operational keepsake.

Going back up was easier than coming down. I forgot my fear of being interred under the sea, and by now my eyes had adjusted to the dark, allowing me more clearly to see the Lilliputian figures chopping away in the narrow mineshafts. I sympathized with these miners whose trade union I was trying to penetrate. One miner had even shared his lunch and presented me with a token of friendship, and for the first time I felt uneasy about having traded on a bogus black-lung father to gain their confidence.

When the train came out of the tunnel into the sunlight, I realized I had to put these misgivings aside and concentrate on the task at hand.

Agent

Since this story is based entirely on facts, the author feels it is his duty not to overstep the bounds of the verifiable, to resist at all costs the perils of invention.

—PAUL AUSTER, *The New York Trilogy*

The agent is the soul of an operation. The intelligence agent, unlike the travel, insurance, or real estate agent, is not paid on a commission basis. He carries out missions on behalf of his case officer, who is also his paymaster unless the agent is working for the cause pro bono.

There are no standard criteria for an agent, unlike West Pointers, whose physical measurements ensure symmetry on the parade ground. Agents are a mixed bag of unemployed and professionals, chambermaids, sailors, cabinet ministers, shipping magnates, guerrilla leaders, mistresses, and musicians.

Even blue-blooded and aristocratic agents are not socially acceptable. They see themselves working for a noble cause, but their self-esteem is not shared by outsiders except in the Soviet Union, where spying is an honorable profession.

The intelligence agent has to be continually vetted. When one agent submits a report, another agent is often tasked to steal a document to confirm the information or plant a "bug" to corroborate it. A political action agent may be assigned to write an editorial for an "agent-of-influence" to act on. Meanwhile, another agent, a counterspy, keeps on the lookout for "doubles" and hostile penetrations.

For most, an agent's life is dangerous and often life threatening, but he normally is not entitled to social security or a pension. In exceptional cases, however, an agent may be given the option of early retirement or granted "resettlement." But the latter is a rare exception.

Kanto was an ideal agent candidate. He had "access," because his brother was the secretary general of the target organization. He was dedicated to democratic ideals and opposed to fascism or communism. Most important, he was unemployed, a university graduate, and needed money.

The trip to Owata would last two weeks, long enough to work up a "soft pitch."

—ɯ—

Kanto and I spent most of our time calling on local union officials, talking to miners, and visiting families. At night we stayed in small Bushidan inns, *ryokan*. Breakfast was a foul-smelling fish soup, lunch was rice balls and seaweed, and for supper we ate squid. Kanto taught me the proper way to belch and end the meal with a *kotowaza*, a Bushidan proverb. My favorite was, "Bushi wa, kuwa nedo, taka yoji." Even if the samurai's stomach is empty, he holds his toothpick high.

After supper we soaked in a hot bath until a blind masseur came to knead out our knots and cramps. Then we talked. I took mental notes as he told me about his childhood and early youth, education, and friends. I probed as deeply as I could, trying to dissect his psychological id without intruding into his Bushidan gestalt.

By the end of our trip, I was ready to risk a "soft pitch."

The Soft Pitch

Dissimulating means drawing a veil composed of honest shadows, which does not constitute falsehood but allows truth some respite.

—UMBERTO ECO, *Island of the Day Before*

Although I was convinced I had elicited enough data about Kanto to risk a soft pitch, I knew that I had to be wary. A foreigner can rarely plumb the Bushidan soul, and I had to tread carefully not to upset Kanto.

After dinner I began by telling Kanto how much I had enjoyed our trip together and that I regretted that it had to come to an end. Kanto agreed, saying he too was sad our time together was almost over. Having provided the opening I was looking for, I asked Kanto if he would like to continue our association after we returned to Edo. I wanted to finish my project and needed someone to help me cobble together more material for the book, which would be hard to obtain on my own. I added that I would insist on paying him a stipend for his services.

By offering to pay him, I had peeled off one layer of my cover. Kanto recoiled as if I had slapped or insulted him, and I wondered if I had misjudged the depth of our friendship. I knew Bushidans don't like mixing money and friendship, but at some point I had to push the money button to move the operation forward. I tried to sugarcoat the offer of money by telling Kanto I couldn't ask him to work for me without offering him a "stipend," stipend being less offensive than "pay" or "salary." Kanto visibly relaxed when I explained the distinction between stipend and salary but stiffened again when I added that the stipend wouldn't be coming out of my pocket but would be paid by my "sponsor."

"Sponsor?" Kanto was on his guard again as I peeled off another layer of my cover. If Kanto would accept a stipend coming from an unidentified sponsor, it would edge him one step closer to recruitment.

I explained to Kanto that a sponsor was necessary to fund research on my book about the coal miners. Kanto scratched his head and shifted uneasily. He looked around the room as if trying to find an answer to his dilemma. He must have decided, because he finally stopped fidgeting, looked at me, and said, "*Daijobu desu*. OK." He would accept my offer of a stipend, because he wouldn't be taking my money and we could still remain friends.

He was right. We would remain friends. I would, however, also be his paymaster. He had accepted the soft pitch. The first hook was in.

The Recruitment

After returning to Edo, Kanto began working for me full time. I asked him to prepare papers for me on the history of the Bushidan labor movement and an analysis of Bushidan labor laws, both nonsensitive tasks. To break him out of his research cocoon, I slipped in a request for a list of labor unions and their officers.

He balked at this request, asking why I needed that kind of information for a book about coal miners. I said something about our leaders needing good information to make wise decisions, information that wasn't always in libraries or archives, information that would provide better understanding about motivations behind the protests against our bases.

It was too much of a stretch for Kanto, and he left the office without saying whether or not he would prepare the report.

We were to have lunch later in the week at a noodle restaurant in Shibuya. I had gotten Kanto used to "clandestine" meetings outside the office and persuaded him to use an alias (he selected Momotaro, the Peach Boy). However, I wasn't sure he would show up, because he hadn't been happy about providing the list of names and had left the office in a bad mood. He was at the restaurant there, however, when I arrived. He slurped down the last of his noodles, nodded briefly, and handed me an envelope. He then got up and left the restaurant. The biographic sketches were inside the envelope. The second hook was in.

The following week I gave Kanto his stipend and asked him to sign a receipt.

"Receipt? First I give you information about my friends. Now you want a receipt for my stipend. Why?"

This was the toughest hurdle, asking a prospective agent to sign for money. I tried to soften the request, saying it was purely an "administrative detail." Since my sponsor's funds came from the government, he had to account for his expenditures. Nothing personal.

I had peeled off the last layer, revealing that Kanto would indirectly be working for the U.S. government. To my surprise, he didn't protest or even react. He reached over and took the receipt, scratched something at the bottom, and handed it back.

It was the character for bridge. Kanto projected himself as a "bridge" between his country and mine, the bridge between him and me, or maybe just a bridge. It didn't matter. Kanto had signed for money, and the last hook was in.

I had earned my brevet as a case officer.

Agent of Influence

In the sphere of political and revolutionary action . . . the professional spy has every facility to fabricate the very facts themselves, and will spread the double evil of emulation in one direction, and of panic, hasty legislation, unreflecting hate on the other.

—JOSEPH CONRAD, *The Secret Agent*

"Agent of Influence" is a contradiction in terms. People with influence have agents, not vice versa. Historical references to agents of influence would cite eminences grises such as Roosevelt's Harry Hopkins and Tsar Nicolas's Rasputin.

Even though "agent of influence" is a misnomer, it is lodged in the espionage lexicon and remains there. Agents of influence are normally "handled" by station chiefs (COSs), although there are exceptions of such agents that were developed by case officers before they reached their positions of influence.

Handling agents of influence is difficult. They balk at signing receipts, won't write reports, refuse to submit to the polygraph, and accept "guidance" only when it is in their best interest.

One such agent of influence, the prime minister of a Southeast Asian country, had allegedly been recruited by the local station chief. The COS had a porous memory, however, and had to jot intelligence requirements from Headquarters on crib notes. He concealed the notes in his hand, glancing at them to remind him of questions to ask his "agent." The prime minister noticed the COS glancing down at something curled in his hand and ordered his aide to grab the COS's crib notes. A tug of war followed until the aide finally wrested the notes from the COS's palm and handed them to the amused prime minister, who jokingly answered each of the questions for the embarrassed station chief.

I had been tasked to recruit an agent of influence in the labor field. Since agents of influence are usually the preserve of station chiefs, not of junior case officers, it was almost impossible for a minor functionary such as me to even contact, much less recruit, a senior official in a government ministry. When I mentioned this to my chief, he was unsympathetic, saying he didn't have a "pool" of gray-haired or senior citizen case officers. I would have to use my ingenuity. "Grow a beard, pencil in wrinkles, walk with a cane, act like Methuselah!"

The Feather Duster

There is a high blowback potential in agent of influence operations, and I had to be careful selecting my target. I settled on a department chief in the Labor Ministry.

Machano was director of that ministry's liaison section. He had studied briefly at Harvard, and according to the U.S. labor attaché, Machano was a "comer." I asked the attaché to invite him to the next embassy reception.

I was introduced to Machano as a colleague interested in labor affairs, and I handed him one of the cards I had had printed identifying me as a special assistant for labor affairs. Machano gave me one of his cards, and after covering the rise of the Edo Firebirds and the approaching typhoon season, I asked him about the current labor unrest in Bushido. He seemed surprised both at the directness of my question and that the American embassy was interested in the views of a minor official.

Machano said the subject was too complex for discussion at a cocktail party. However, if I was seriously interested in the labor situation, I should come by his office, where we could discuss it in detail.

Having a secretary implies status in Bushido, so I asked the station chief's secretary to phone Machano's office and ask for an appointment. A date and time were settled on, and I arrived at Machano's office carrying a copy of the Congressional Record, which contained minutes of a recent Senate Labor Relations Committee meeting.

We discussed the labor situation for almost an hour before he had to leave for a meeting. Machano apologized for cutting our meeting short and invited me to lunch the following week so we could continue our discussion. I thanked him, leaving behind the "confidential" copy of the Congressional Record.

At the lunch the next week, I told Machano that "senior officials" in Washington had been impressed by his analysis of the labor situation. He seemed surprised that I had reported his views to Washington but was reassured when I told him his comments would be treated as "highly confidential."

After lunch, I invited Machano to dinner at my house when he was free. He seemed reluctant, but he finally accepted when I insisted on reciprocating for his hospitality.

My first objective, making contact and establishing rapport, had been achieved. Moving the relationship forward was going to be more difficult. I was running out of questions and in status-conscious Bushido, it was unlikely that a senior official like Machano would continue to spend time meeting with a minor embassy functionary. I had to elevate my status and convince Machano I was both important and influential.

The plan called for two extra case officers, a car with chauffer, a compliant maid, and a well-rehearsed family. Alex Taketa, a case officer of Bushidan descent, and Paul, a classmate from The Farm, volunteered. I requisitioned two cars from the embassy motor pool, rehearsed the maid, and briefed my family.

The scenario began with a clandestine element. I had told Machano that, "for security reasons," I would pick him up a block away rather than in front of his office. The request puzzled Machano, but he seemed intrigued by my concern for his "security" and agreed to my request.

Alex was standing next to the embassy sedan, flicking his feather duster in good Bushidan style back and forth across the hood. When Machano arrived and got into the car, I pointed to the other sedan pulling out ahead, our security "outrider." I snapped my fingers and the chauffer turned on the radio, which happened to be tuned to the armed forces radio station. I told Machano I often received coded messages over the radio. I clicked my fingers, and the chauffer turned off the radio. I told Machano we could now talk freely, because the chauffer was a deaf-mute.

The charade was almost exposed when we drove up to the house. My son, Gray, rushed out to greet "Uncle Alex," who ducked behind his feather duster. I explained to Machano that the chauffer was like an uncle to my children, then quickly escorted him into the house.

At the front door, the maid announced that there was an "important telephone call from Washington" for me in my study. I excused myself, leaving my wife to escort Machano to the living room for cocktails.

The dinner went smoothly except for interruptions from the maid, who kept announcing phone calls from the ambassador. Finally, worried about over-kill, I slipped into the kitchen and told the maid there was no need for further announcements.

Machano became more relaxed, tousling the children's hair and compliment-
ing Joy on the dinner. When the meal was over, I invited Machano into the study
for cigars and brandy. After discussing the travails of the UN and insurrections in
former European colonies, I touched on the situation in Bushido and the increasing anti-American sentiment there, which was disturbing American government
leaders in Washington. Machano said I had to understand the mind-set of the
Bushidans, the majority of whom were too busy trying to fill their rice bowls to be
anti-American. There was only a small minority that was creating trouble for its
own political ends, but this might be difficult for foreigners to understand.

I refilled Machano's brandy, telling him that he had put his finger on the problem. Our leaders were not that well informed. Bushido was a mystery to many
American leaders, and one of my tasks was to try to unravel the mystery. Bushido
was a complex country, and I needed someone, a Bushidan like Machano, to
help me in keep our decision makers better informed. We could do this working
together "unofficially" behind the scenes.

At this point, Machano raised his eyebrows, dipped his cigar in the brandy
snifter, and looked up at the ceiling. I decided not to press him further, because
the "unofficial" part seemed to bother him. I decided to change the subject, but
before I had a chance, he held up his hand and said, "Mr. St. Martin, let me speak
frankly. The problem you are discussing is one of your own making. Your style
of democracy, which you are encouraging here, guarantees freedom of expression
and freedom of assembly, which presumably includes the kind of demonstrations
you are referring to. Your president should also understand that we are a sover-
eign nation, not an American colony, and my first loyalty is to my country.

"As for our relationship, yours and mine, I am willing to help and cooperate on certain issues. In the future I might even ask you to use your influence
with Washington to resolve certain problems quietly. Again, I must emphasize,
I am speaking about cooperation, not collaboration. I hope you understand the
difference.

"I will pass on to my minister the concerns you have expressed," he said. "I
will not report our conversation tonight, which might be misunderstood."

Machano then toasted to "cooperation and friendship," thanked me for the
dinner, and said goodnight. Alex was waiting with his feather duster and drove
Machano home.

When Alex came back, we sat down for an operational postmortem. Had
Machano really been impressed by the special effects, the outrider cars, the
feather-duster chauffeur, and my alleged "special channel" to the White House?
Perhaps. And even if he saw through the trappings of the charade, at least it made
him feel important.

The "sting" had a least partially succeeded. Although Machano had not been recruited as an agent of influence, he had agreed to continue our relationship and "cooperate" on matters of mutual interest. And Machano also probably thought he had gained something. A back channel to the White House.

Dirty Tricks

It should be noted that children at play are not playing about; their game should be seen as the most serious minded activity.

—MONTAIGNE

In 1958 Bushido hosted an international trade fair in Edo. Communist China, trying to shed its international pariah image, rented the largest pavilion at the fair. As a promotional gimmick and to attract attention, the Chinese embassy distributed two thousand vouchers offering free tea and fortune cookies at their pavilion on opening day.

When an agent turned over one of the vouchers to his case officer, it was seized on as a target of opportunity. The coupon was altered in another agent's print shop to read, "GOOD FOR ONE FREE BOTTLE OF TSINGTAO BEER!" Four thousand copies of the phony vouchers were then distributed throughout Chinatown.

On opening day thousands of Bushidans and Chinese waving the "free beer" vouchers descended on the Red China pavilion. The surprised Chinese behind the stand tried vainly to stem the onrush, offering free tea and biscuits. The crowd however, egged on by Station agent-provocateurs, stormed through the Chinese pavilion, leaving it in a shambles, before the police finally arrived to restore order just as another agent arrived to take pictures that appeared in the paper the next day over the caption "Red Chinese come up empty."

Headquarters suggested getting back to more serious business.

My second tour in Edo was nearing an end. We had been living in a small village on the outskirts of Edo, home to Bushidan film stars, the president of the world's largest soy sauce company, and a U.S. Air Force general who enjoyed playing "pass-the-orange" with local mama-sans.

My family had grown by two. Gray was born in 1955, Megan in 1958, both in St. Luke's Hospital in Edo. Laurie attended a Bushidan kindergarten, and Kent played to the hilt his role of "first son" at the Koi No Bori (Boy's Day) festival.

In late June 1958, my chief handed me a cable from Headquarters requesting a French-speaking case officer for a priority program in Cham. The cable added that St. Martin had been nominated. Following home leave, St. Martin was to report to Headquarters for "reading in" before his onward assignment to Cham.

I told the chief a college minor in French hardly qualified me as a "French speaker." He told me not to worry. "Down there they just use the infinitive *'Aller, manger, pisser.' Bon Chance*, St. Martin!"

CHAPTER 5: **Covert Action**

What is this, the sound and rumor? What is this that all men hear,
Like the wind in hollow valleys when the storm is drawing near?
—WILLIAM MORRIS, "The March of the Workers"

Preliminaries to wars, the diplomatic shadow boxing, demarches, mobiliza-tions, and ultimatums have remained unchanged, although they have been broadened recently to include UN resolutions, embargoes, sanctions, and nuclear blackmail.

The nature of war has, however, changed. Carpet bombing, claymore mines, carrier-launched Poseidons, and nuclear missiles have relegated cavalry charges and trench warfare to the dustbins of history. [Patriotic calls to "rally round the flag" fall on deaf ears or have been drowned out by chants of "hell no, we won't go!" The quest for combat, however, has not slaked.] Bugles may be muted and cannons mothballed, but the warhorses in Washington, Moscow, and Beijing still neigh and paw the ground, cocking their ears toward the rumbling in the dis-tance, the muffled echoes of covert action.

Covert action is not new. Homer's wooden horse in *The Iliad*, the bogus "Ems Dispatch" sparking the Franco-Prussian War, the phony plans for the Allied inva-sion planted on a floating corpse, the abduction of Stalin's daughter, and the Bay of Pigs are noteworthy precedents.

Covert action provides ideal stomping grounds for restless combatants. Outdoor rings feature brawling dissidents flailing at bobbing and weaving oppo-nents. Inside the tent, plotters hatch cabals and power-hungry colonels ready coups d'etat. Meanwhile, currency manipulators, influence peddlers, arms mer-chants, and case officers stir the cauldron.

Covert action stage props include clandestine radios, portable printing presses, Kalashnikovs, rocket launchers, and plastic explosives.

Financial backers of covert action prefer to remain anonymous.

Covert action flies various flags of convenience: counterinsurgency, antiter-rorism, and nation building. The latter has a particularly good ring to it, offering a cloak of respectability. Agency officers are skilled in covert action, particularly "nation building," where such skills as developing rapport, instilling confidence, and injecting enthusiasm stand them in good stead. Having ample supplies, arms, and funds to draw on also helps.

The Agency has a mixed nation-building record, lauded for toppling unsavory dictators like Mohammad Mossadegh and castigated for its alleged role in assassinating the Congo's Patrice Lumumba and the overthrow of Chile's Salvador Allende.

Cham was the Agency's covert-action Thermopylae.*

---

* Battle in 480 BC, when a small force of Spartans fought to the last man, holding off the entire Persian army.

CHAPTER 6:
Cham, Nation Building

We were a self-centered army without parade or gesture, devoted to freedom . . . a purpose so ravenous that it devoured all our strength, a hope so transcendent that our earlier ambitions faded in its glare.

—T. E. LAWRENCE, *Seven Pillars of Wisdom*

Bards recounting the idylls of the Agency will dwell on Cham, where, in unequaled acts of courage and despair, the CIA had its finest hour.

The idyll began in the summer of 1959. Clutching Langley's guidons, we rode into Cham. Our motives and expectations, illusory and naive as they may have been, were in joint with the time. Cham was "our oyster," and we believed we could make a difference there. It was a young country, unencumbered by ancient régimes, Hapsburg intrigues, or Bourbon plots.

Cham was a political action frontier, where we shed cloaks and daggers for civic action garb and nation-building tool kits. We operated in the open, because there was little cover, no place to hide, no secrets that wouldn't come out, no "plausible denial."

During the late 1950s, the Cold War was at its height. In Washington the prevailing doctrine, promulgated by John Foster Dulles, secretary of state and brother of CIA director Allen Dulles, was that the Soviet Union and Communist China were plotting the takeover of Southeast Asia. The doctrine that, if one Southeast Asian country fell to the communists, the others would soon topple became known as the "Domino Theory."

The Geneva settlement in 1954 had already opened the door to the communist takeover of North Vietnam. To stem the tide, the United States sent arms and advisers to shore up South Vietnam. The other country in the way of the communists was Cham.

In 1950 the newly elected U.S. president, wary of being drawn into a war in Southeast Asia, affirmed support for the "neutrality" of Cham. At the same time, the North Vietnamese stepped up their covert operations. The "Red Prince" Souphong, had earlier been imprisoned by the Cham government until he escaped with his jailers to North Vietnam, reinfiltrated Cham, and set up his base in his home province of Sap Neua.

The communist incursions set off alarm bells in Washington and resurrected the Domino Theory. J. Campbell, an Agency officer, told me he had been summoned to a briefing in 1959 in the director's office. According to Campbell, Allen Dulles, standing in front of a map of Asia pointing to Cham, said, "Gentlemen, there's a fire burning out there!"*

Allen Dulles had fired the starting gun in the race to save Southeast Asia.

The Land of a Million Elephants

Time, as we all know, is sometimes a bird on the wing, and sometimes a crawling worm, but men are happiest when oblivious of time's quick or slow pace.

—W. TREVOR, *Reading Turgenev*

Cham is landlocked, isolated, and backward. Its people are laid back, gentle, and easygoing. Most of the country is mountainous, although there are two sprawling plains, one in the north and one in the south.

The northern plain is a broad steppe, ringed by obsidian cliffs and covered with elephant grass. Huge prehistoric urn-shaped boulders lie scattered over this Asian Stonehenge, known as La Plaine des Jarres, the Plain of Jars. The savanna to the south was the former hunting preserve of Cham satraps and French gouverneurs. Elephants still lumber across the plain under watchful eyes of wild boars, buffalo, and tigers.

The lowland Cham who inhabit the valleys are Buddhists and survive on sticky rice. These valley dwellers are peaceful and lethargic except during the equinox or summer solstice, when the advent of fertility rites turn them into frenzied Cham copulators.

The highlanders, or montagnards, live in thatched stilted huts on slash-and-burn plots that have been hacked out of the surrounding forest. Fierce warriors, they hunt with crossbows and drink fermented wine. Their staple crop is the opium poppy.

Cham has two capitals. The seat of government is in Viensiang, a sleepy town lying along the Mekong River across from neighboring Thailand. The royal capital, Luang Prabat, is up in the mountains and, at the time I lived there, boasted the world's only monarch who drove a Ford Edsel.

That the Cham are fatalists is not surprising. Their country has been invaded by tribes of Mongols, Chinese hordes, Vietnamese marauders, and the French, die-hard colonials backed by their Foreign Legion.

---

* Campbell alleged he spent the next ten years "pissing on it."

In 1954 the French were defeated by Ho Chi Minh's Vietminh at Dien Bien Phu and Cham became an independent country. Unfortunately, its borders as well as those of Vietnam and Cambodia, were drawn by European bureaucrats, and this explains why the people of Cham have no sense of a "national identity."

Henry

That glorious vision of doing good, which is so often the sanguine marriage of so many good minds, arose before him, and he even saw himself in the illusion of some influence.

—CHARLES DICKENS, *Tale of Two Cities*

That there was even a Station in bucolic Cham was an anomaly. Only when the KGB set up shop in Viensiang did the CIA decide to follow suit. The small espionage outpost remained an operational backwater until the arrival of its new station chief, Henry.

Henry was an old European hand who had several operational coups to his credit, including the tunnel under East Berlin and the defrocking of a KGB station chief. Eventually, Henry tired of Europe, where most of his case officers were OSS retreads and their agents shopworn refugees and unsavory defectors. When Henry heard about the opening in Viensiang, he sensed the country was an operational lode waiting to be mined and volunteered for the post.

Detractors at Headquarters were concerned that Henry's Teutonic character would grate on the easygoing Cham. The director, however, an old friend of Henry's, was confident the dynamic Prussian would win over even the lethargic Cham.

Henry caused a stir shortly after he arrived. Instead of keeping a "low profile," he let the Cham know his office was open for business. Clients began coming to his door, and Henry soon developed a number of government officials and young army officers.

Henry's openness with the Cham grated on the American ambassador, a corpulent political appointee who took great pride in his karate black belt, which he hung on the wall behind his desk. It irritated the ambassador that Henry lived outside Viensiang on the airport road, which made it difficult to contact him on short notice.

The electricity outside Viensang was erratic and unreliable, and Henry had a backup generator installed at his house. When the Chinese madam who ran "the house" next door asked Henry to leave his generator on at night for her late clients, Henry agreed. And in return for letting her tap into his generator, he asked her to provide information on some of her clients.

Henry lived on the airport road for only a few months before the ambassador ordered him to move into town nearer the embassy. Henry had no choice, and he turned his house over to a newly arrived case officer and his wife, Brenda Lou, a strict Southern Baptist, who had only agreed to come to Cham to protect her husband from Asian fleshpots.

Her husband was often away on field trips, and Brenda Lou became increasingly irritated at the noise from the generator in the shed out back. One night the throbbing noise so infuriated Brenda Lou that she stomped out to the shed and threw the switch to shut off the generator.

Unbeknownst to Brenda Lou, she plunged the entire airport road into darkness. The tap from the generator to the madam's "house" was only one of a series of taps into the line by noodle and cigarette shops along the airport road, the last tap at the Buddhist temple Wat Phrasay faintly lighting the one lamp flickering above the inner courtyard.

The morning after Brenda Lou threw the switch, an angry saffron-robed monk, the "Venerable Bonze" from the Buddhist wat on the airport road, stormed into the ambassador's office in the embassy. Rapping his cane on the floor, the Venerable Bonze berated the ambassador for shutting off power to a Buddhist shrine while the monks were praying.

The ambassador assured the bonze he would take action. He called Henry in and told him to turn that "damn generator" back on and leave it on!

Henry later claimed credit for the most successful electrical power project since the TVA (Tennessee Valley Authority).

More serious matters lay ahead for Henry. In 1959 the slumbering Cham were again rousted from their hibernation. Armed Pathet Cham cadre, trained in North Vietnam, were infiltrating into northern Cham. With little government presence in the area, the infiltrations went unreported until an alert outpost commander picked up "bamboo telegraph" clackings announcing the "return of our brothers from the North."

The clackings were reported to Viensiang, and Henry's military intelligence contact briefed him on the reports. Henry cabled the gist of the report to Headquarters, flagging it for the director's attention. Henry added his own comment that the report was evidence that the Pathet Cham intended to gain control of Cham. It would achieve this goal by infiltrating Moscow-trained cadre into Cham, establishing bases in the two northern provinces to serve as springboards to take over the whole of Cham. Henry concluded, "The Cham government, still weak from a bungled French Caesarean and viral Marxist infection, was paralyzed and unable to take action to remedy its maladies since it was run by 'colonial leftovers.'"

Henry concluded that only a hard-hitting political action program could save Cham.

Headquarters, accustomed to dramatic pronouncements from Henry, usually treated them as "wolf cries" from a pastured-out station chief. In reply to this latest cable, Headquarters insisted Henry provide details on numbers of armed Pathet Cham cadre, specific routes and infiltration points, and evidence that North Vietnam and the USSR were providing aid to the Pathet Cham.

Henry's detractors had not, however, taken into account the director's reaction to Henry's cable. Allen Dulles had a high regard for Henry, as both had entered the Agency around the same time. Both men had distinguished themselves in World War II, Dulles brokering peace talks with Galeazzo Ciano, Benito Mussolini's son-in-law, and Henry spiriting nuclear scientists out of Germany.

Henry's cable intrigued the director, who called the Far East Division chief and asked for an immediate briefing on Cham.

Prior to the director's phone call, there had been little interest in the land-locked kingdom in former Indochina. When the division chief called Friedman, the Headquarters officer responsible for Cham, and told him to report to the director's office to give a briefing, Friedman ran up all seven flights of stairs to the director's office.

Allen Dulles sat behind a long, curved mahogany desk, flanked on either side by American and CIA flags. Friedman, without waiting for instructions, went directly to the director's desk and unrolled a map of Cham. He anchored the corners of the map with opium weights Henry had sent shortly after his arrival in Cham.

Friedman pointed out the two provinces in question and the infiltration routes highlighted by Magic Marker lightning bolts. Dulles pored over the map, then asked Friedman about the political situation, the capability of the Cham army, the reliability of Cham intelligence sources, and the practicability of mounting operations in a country as backward and underdeveloped as Cham.

The director, impressed with Friedman's briefing, turned to the director of operations and told him to put Cham on the "front burner." He would go over and brief the president, who would undoubtedly want to know what our agency was going to do about it.

I was later told that after Dulles briefed the president on the situation in Cham, the president commented, "Those damned Soviet locusts are on the move again, and they'll be descending on Hawaii soon if we don't stop them. Get that outfit of yours cracking. I don't want some half-assed Asian country blowing up in my face!"

Henry enjoyed being in the eye of the storm. He had gotten the green light to come up with a political action program and had already drafted his cable proposing to assist the Cham to establish a national "rice-roots" political organization, with chapters in villages and hamlets throughout Cham, to support civic action projects such as digging wells and setting up dispensaries, to organize hamlet militia, and to recruit and train political action and psychological warfare cadre to support the program. He added that four additional case officers would be required.

Although there was a certain amount of grousing at Headquarters about the "snake-oil charlatan" and his program, the grumbling was muted. A task force was organized and a message sent canvassing for case officer candidates.

In less than a month Henry's "four horsemen" had been nominated and were at Headquarters "reading in."

There wasn't that much to "read in" on. Material on Cham was sparse, limited to dated issues of the *National Geographic*, foreign missionary memoirs, French military dispatches, and extracts from the *Congressional Record* documenting abuses of the U.S. AID (Agency for International Development) program, the *Record* alleging that licenses issued for importing Caterpillar tractors had been altered to permit the import of Mercedes Benz. The result was that Viensiang boasted more Mercedes per capita than Stuttgart did.

Bt the end of June, we four case officers requested by Henry had finished "reading in" and were on our way to the Land of a Million Elephants.

—⁘—

Henry was shorter than I had expected. His jocular face was contrasted by a Teutonic jaw, and his piercing eyes warned against trifling.

Henry was in a good mood, having just come from a verbal sparring session with "the great white whale," as he referred to the ambassador. Henry didn't waste any time. After welcoming us to the Station, he briefed us on the program we were to implement. He emphasized that the program would not really be "covert," because the term had little meaning in Cham, where there were no secrets. In Cham everything was out in the open and tradecraft was useless. The Cham political action program was couched as "nation building" and "civic action."

Henry said that, with the exception of the Pathet Cham, all of the political organizations and parties in Cham were tattered colonial relics. We would have to start from scratch and create a national rice-roots organization with chapters in every province, district, and village. It was a tall order, and Henry said he counted on us being up to the task.

"To teach you the finer points of raw political action and bare-knuckles politics, a former Chicago ward boss and Agency consultant, is arriving tomorrow. He will instruct you in the techniques of dead voter registration, ballot box switching, and making use of the pork barrel, or in the case of Cham, the rice crock. He is also an expert on precinct organization, how to organize the local population and ensure getting them all out to vote on election day. Chicago may not be Phu Khat or Phong Saly, but the techniques of political organization are universal, and what works in Chicago and Peoria can work in Viensiang and Pat Peng."

Henry then went over to the map of Cham tacked on the wall of his office. He said we would be playing catch-up to a well-organized Pathet Cham political action program already under way. With his pointer, he indicated the red areas on the map. These were controlled by the Pathet Cham, and, at least for the time being, we could forget about them. The areas shaded in blue were population centers such as Viensiang and Pak Boun, which were more or less pro-government. We should encourage the Cham to set up chapters and do some organizing, but not spend too much time there. "I want you to concentrate on the green areas, the villages and hamlets in the countryside that are neutral or noncommitted. Color that area blue!"

It was a fiery pep talk from our Bavarian Knute Rockne. Now it was game time.

Vienna

Vienna wasn't a crisis Station. A few double agents, defectors, and information peddlers claiming the Russians were dumping nuclear waste into the Blue Danube. Vienna was often referred to as the "Lederhosen" post.

One night Peer, the station chief in Vienna, was called in by his communications officer for an "OPERATIONAL IMMEDIATE" from Headquarters. Peer read the cable twice, then summoned his case officers to his office.

Peer was standing in front of his desk, waving a cable at the five groggy case officers who sat in front of him. "What I want each of you to tell me is why, yes, why all your contacts seem to be unaware of what's going on in this Austrian paradise they live in. Are they so full of beer and apple strudel that they are sleeping through the biggest crisis in this country since World War II? The entire Red Army could be marching down Lindenstrasse and I have to hear about it from Headquarters!

"I have just been advised by Langley that significant numbers of political action cadre, armed and trained in Moscow, are at this very moment infiltrating this Hapsburgian kingdom through mountain passes and river valleys! I want you to roust your contacts from their hibernation and have them find out about these infiltrations!"

The sleepy-eyed and puzzled case officers looked like chastened school-boys whose knuckles had just been cracked. Peer was still waving the cable at them when the communications officer burst into his office. "Sorry, sir. It was a mistake. The cable was sent to Viensiang and was routed to Vienna by mistake. One of those communications glitches. Headquarters says they're sorry for any inconvenience."

Peer sent his befuddled case officers back to bed. His curiosity had been aroused, however, and he reread the cable with its references to black-pajama cadre, pirogues, buffalo carts, and panji-staked trails. He put the cable down and went over to the world globe standing next to his desk. He spun it several times looking for this "Viensiang" without success and finally gave up, deciding to try the *Rand-McNally* the next day.

Boostershot

All events in history reappear in one fashion or another . . . the first time as tragedy, the second as farce.

—KARL MARX

Henry's wasn't Cham's first political action program. Two years before his arrival, the American embassy's "Country Team" had come up with Operation Boostershot, a program that had gone badly wrong.

The program centered around two Caterpillar tractors that had been gathering dust in an Agency for International Development (AID) warehouse. The plan called for airdropping the tractors into two districts controlled by the Pathet Cham. The pro-government candidates would take credit for bringing in the two tractors and the grateful villagers would express their gratitude at the polls on election day. The Country Team planners forgot, however, that Cham was a security sieve and the plan was bound to leak.

Rumors that a plane would be arriving had spread quickly through the two districts, and when the C-130 appeared, a crowd had already gathered on the ground. The first plane flew over and dropped the crate with the tractor inside attached to two parachutes. When the crate hit the ground, the Pathet Cham candidate rushed out shouting, "Look! The 'peoples' tractor' the Pathet Cham has gotten for you! With it you can build roads and plow new fields. Long live the Pathet Cham."

The villagers ran out onto the field, trampling over the hapless pro-government candidate still holding his prepared speech. When the crowd reached the gigantic crate, they ripped it open, revealing the bright yellow tractor. They climbed over it, stroking the silver smokestack, pulling levers, running their hands over the tracks. The Pathet Cham leader climbed onto the seat and pressed the starter button. Puffs of blue smoke belched from the exhaust as the engine caught and the tractor lurched forward, heading across the field. The government candidate, picking himself off the ground, had no doubt about who was driving his tractor.

The performance was repeated in the second district, the Pathet Cham candidate again taking credit for the yellow "manna from the sky."

Both Pathet Cham candidates won by a landslide. Boostershot was consigned to the shredder.

Henry called the Country Team meetings "The Ambassador's Amateur Hour." He had no intention of giving a briefing on his program. He was required, however, to keep the ambassador informed about all nonintelligence operations in which his people were involved. So, Henry told the ambassador his people were working with the Cham on a "civic action program." Its objective was to help the Cham in "strengthening their democratic institutions."

The ambassador suspected there was more to the program than Henry told him, but he couldn't quarrel with "fostering democracy."

The Young Turks

Henry had already begun laying the groundwork for his political action program before we arrived, organizing evening seminars for young Cham army officers and government officials, Cham's "Young Turks" fed up with the "Francophile gerontocracy" running their country. Henry worked these seminars like revival meetings, lashing out at communism and corruption, extolling freedom and democracy. He told his audience they were tomorrow's leaders and should start thinking about what they could do for their country.

The night Henry introduced us to his group; the theme was "political organization." He agreed with their concerns about the country stagnating because it was run by what they referred to as stale, colonial leftovers. Cham was a new country and needed new blood, new ideas, and a new political organization. Henry, after telling the group he thought the leaders of such an organization were here tonight, excused himself and left the room.

A lively discussion followed until General Ouane Rathikone got up to speak. "Henry's right. We have to organize a political movement of all the Cham and have soldiers and civilians working together in the interests of the country. We could call it the Cham Union Banda Solidaire, CUBS."

Ouane had gotten the group's attention, and they all started talking at once among themselves. The general was a good speaker and a popular figure. The betel-nut chewing army chief of staff, a former sergeant in the French maquis, had been expelled from St. Cyr, the French military academy, for referring to his instructors as "wooden-headed officers with Dien Bien Phu complexes."

I was surprised to hear the rough ex-sergeant speak so eloquently about the need for a "national movement" and even giving it such a high-sounding name. Then I remembered Henry telling us about his "very good friend" General Ouane, and I knew where his inspiration for the CUBS had come from.

When Ouane finished, Phousat stood up and nominated General Ouane for CUBS president. The group clapped and someone seconded the nomination. Then another member of the group stood up and nominated Lieutenant Colonel Oudone as CUBS vice president. This nomination was also applauded and seconded.

I was sure Henry was pleased at this demonstration "of political action in the raw," but I saw that he seemed upset and had taken Ouane aside out of earshot of the others. When Ouane returned, he took the floor again, this time nominating Impeng Soolay, a minor official in the ministry of information, as secretary general. After brief applause and seconding of Impeng, Oudone nominated Ciao Sopsana, a schoolteacher from Luang Prabat, as treasurer. The nominations were then closed.

Henry was breathing easier. With two leadership positions filled by civilians, he couldn't be accused of midwifing a military junta.

The newly elected leaders would be our counterparts in the nation-building program. We became inseparable, in and out of each other's homes, sharing sticky rice and mosquito nets, running together when the enemy wasn't far behind. This intimacy affected our objectivity and often blindsided us from seeing cracks in the program until too late to stanch them. There was a tendency to get caught up in a "we-are-winning" hubris.

When we finally severed ties, the scars never healed.

My counterpart was Lieutenant Colonel Oudone, whose uncle was a high official in the ancien régime. His uncle had little use for the upstart CUBS even though his nephew was a vice president.

Oudone was an optimist by nature, a quality that had its downside, however. He always looked on the bright side of our nation-building activities, often misleading me into thinking we were making progress when the opposite was the case. He didn't want to upset me by confronting me with problems, figuring they would eventually take care of themselves. His *Bo penh yang*—it doesn't matter—philosophy was typically Cham. When I confronted him about rumored "paper"

CUBS chapters, he brushed aside my concerns. If I asked him about allegations that military commanders were forcing village chiefs to establish CUBS chapters, he replied they were only helping to "color Henry's map blue."

Betsy Ross

Oudone and I were watching the sun, with its canvas of reds and oranges, set over the Mekong, when our reverie was interrupted by Bon Xou, his wife. Madame Oudone, wearing the traditional Cham gold-embroidered sarong, glided noiselessly around the house, rarely interrupting our conversations. I was surprised when I looked up and saw Bon Xou standing in front of us, arms crossed and scowling.

"I overheard you talking about the Cham not being patriotic. What do you expect? Until a few years ago, Cham didn't even exist as a country. All most Cham remember is being ruled by the French, and unlike Vietnam and China, Cham has no modern heroes like Ho Chi or Mao to look up to!

"Cham does, however, have a good flag, red with three white elephants with their trunks entwined. Most Cham don't know what their flag looks like, unless they've seen faded remnants of flags flying over government buildings or military outposts.

"Why don't you have the CUBS distribute Cham flags throughout Cham, a flag for every village? Have the CUBS sponsor ceremonies, with the village chiefs given the honor of raising the flag."

Oudone and I sat spellbound, with our mouths open, listening to the normally reticent Bon Xou. She wasn't finished.

"The Cham Women's Association, of which I am president, will make the flags if St. Martin can get us some sewing machines and bolts of red and white denim cloth. With twenty-five Singer sewing machines and two hundred bolts of cloth, in a month we can make enough flags to fly over all the villages in Cham!"

Bon Xou's proposal was the most practical one I had heard since coming to Cham. I told her we would try to get the sewing machines and bolts of red and white denim cloth.

Al, our logistics officer, was always glad to have an excuse to go to Bangkok. He liked scouring the markets along the klongs (canals) during the day and visiting the local massage parlors at night. He left for Bangkok two days after Bon Xou had proposed the flag project. He sent out word to his Chinese contacts for them to come up with twenty-five Singer sewing machines and two hundred bolts of red and two hundred bolts of white denim cloth. Within forty-eight hours, his order had been filled. The sewing machines and cloth were flown to Viensiang on a Dakota C-47 and then trucked to the headquarters of the Cham Women's Association.

Several weeks later I went by the warehouse where the flags were being made. I had begun to have second thoughts about my enthusiasm for the project, because I had been in Cham long enough not to expect too much when it came to Cham productivity. I had underestimated Bon Xou, however. The warehouse was throbbing with the hum of pumping treadles. Bon Xou was sitting out front, facing two rows of sewing machines being operated by her colleagues in the Cham Women's Association. If the rhythm of the throbbing machines slacked off or was interrupted, Bon Xou would immediately look up and search out the offender. She would then stare the culprit down and wait until the humming rhythm resumed.

Seamstresses on one side of the big room hemmed the squares of red cloth, and after finishing, handed them across the aisle to the other row of seamstresses, who would stitch on the precut elephant patterns. When they were finished their final stitching, young girl runners took the finished flags to the rear of the warehouse and tied them into bundles.

It was a mass production operation that would have made Henry Ford proud, turning out more than a hundred flags a week. The flag operation almost blew when a journalist, who had come to see me at my house in Viensiang, noticed a file of Cham women passing through my screened porch, depositing bundles of flags at one end of the porch. When the journalist asked me about the flags, I replied offhandedly that my hobby was collecting flags from different countries. He commented dryly that my collection was probably the largest in East Asia.

In Every Village

Oudone and I spent most of our time on trips to the various provinces, setting up CUBS chapters. During these visits, I tried to stay in the background, although in a Cham village it was impossible for me to "blend in" or keep a low profile.

Oudone's routine rarely varied. He would begin by presenting the village chief with a petit pistolet, a 38-caliber "Saturday night special" that was the best rapport builder in our civic action kit. The village chief would then assemble the villagers so Oudone could make a speech about the CUBS. His speeches met with blank stares until he presented the village with a community radio set, which he immediately tuned to Radio Viensiang and a popular song program. He would then offer a medical kit to the village shaman, a box of school supplies for the local teacher, and CUBS pins, the Station having ordered fifty thousand CUBS pins from an enterprising tinsmith in Bangkok. The pins were worn as earrings, breechclout fasteners, or as hair ornaments.

The finale was the presentation of the flag, which the village chief would raise up the newly erected village flagpole. In the evening, there would be a CUBS-sponsored roast pig barbecue. Following the inauguration of each new CUBS chapter, Henry would add another pin to his map.

The Moh Lam

Another political action vehicle was the Moh Lam team, a Cham creation that was very effective. The Moh Lam were itinerant actors and troubadours who traveled through the villages in remote mountainous regions.

The Moh Lam team would enter one of these isolated villages and distribute balloons, trinkets, and rice balls while performing juggling acts and magic tricks. They would put on puppet shows for the children in the afternoon while awaiting the return of the villagers working in the rice fields. In the evening, the Moh Lam would put on a play, one usually casting the Pathet Cham as villains and evil predators raiding hamlets and carrying off the village chief's daughter. The play climaxed with the CUB warriors dramatically coming to her rescue.

The Moh Lam teams were popular with both Cham and montagnard audiences, but their success was short-lived. The Pathet Cham began retaliating against villages that had welcomed the Moh Lam teams, burning huts, carrying off livestock, taking hostages, and in several cases, executing Moh Lam team leaders.

Without security, the teams were forced to limit their performances to secure areas where they were less needed as a propaganda weapon. The teams were eventually disbanded.

The Rally

The *walk-about* was a dance where folks stood around in a semi-circle . . . and dance, dance the human-being story, however that story was, however that story felt and however you wanted to dance it, while everybody else watched.
—T. SPANBAUER, *The Man Who Fell in Love with the Moon*

The Pathet Cham retaliated, not only against the Moh Lam teams but also against the villages where the CUBS had set up chapters. They burned flags, smashed village radio sets, and ripped off CUBS pins in areas where the there was little security and no Cham army presence.

The escalation of Pathet Cham attacks in areas where the CUBS had apparently been making inroads caused some concern in Washington. Something had to be done to reinvigorate the political action program. Headquarters suggested a CUBS political rally.

Henry resisted the idea at first, contending that rallies and demonstrations were not in the Cham tradition and the foreign hand would show. Henry changed his mind, however, when one of his case officers suggested that if the rally was tied into the popular fertility festival, it would have a good chance of success.

The solstice fertility festival was the most popular annual event in Cham. A wooden phallus fifty feet high was erected in the center of the marketplace. Revelers doused themselves with Tiger Balm oil and reptile aphrodisiacs and danced around the marketplace and through the town, throwing buckets of water at stall keepers and passersby. The dancing and merrymaking went on for three days, revelers making their way down to the riverbank at sunset, where they gyrated and copulated to the rhythm of thumping tom-toms, "climaxing" as the skyrockets burst overhead.

Filipino technicians helped the CUBS in their preparations for the rally. A twenty-foot neon sign, powered by a portable generator, was erected on a sandbar in the middle of the Mekong. The sign flashed the Cham letters C-U-B-S, in sequence and then all together.

The blinking lights flashed into the Soviet ambassador's bedroom fronting on the river, and he protested to the Cham foreign minister about the neon intrusion into his sleeping quarters. The foreign minister shrugged off the protest, telling the ambassador that the sign had become a popular evening attraction for the Cham who gathered along the riverbank to watch the flashing neon display.

The rally was set to coincide with the final day of the fertility festival, when the crowds would be the largest. The plan called for hundreds of CUBS cadre to assemble near the giant phallus, march through the marketplace, and end up at the Salle de Fete, the grand hall where French colonials danced their minuets on Bastille Day. The plan called for General Ouane to make a speech from the dais erected in front of the Salle.

CUBS cadre assembled and then marched off carrying cardboard placards condemning CORRUPTION (caricatures of fat Vietnamese merchants handing out wads of the local currency) and COMMUNISM (fang-toothed Pathet Cham with hammers and sickles tattooed on their buttocks). The column marching to the Salle was swelled by hundreds of revelers who fell in with the CUBS marchers.

A seasonal downpour interrupted the parade briefly, causing some of the placards to run, but the sun soon reappeared and the march continued. Arriving at La Salle de Fetes, the CUBS cadre dutifully piled their placards in front of the dais, where General Ouane stood waiting to speak.

Ouane was a natural orator and a popular figure with the Cham. He began by welcoming the crowd and then announced it was too bad the Pathet Cham couldn't make it to the rally, because of an epidemic of the "shrinking organ disease" in their villages. The crowd roared its approval, prompting Ouane to poke more fun at the "Pathetic Pathets" before leading into the main theme about the CUBS.

Ouane extolled the CUBS as an organization that would BURN out corruption and communism! The word "BURN" was the signal for two CUBS cadre to light their torches and apply them to the pile of placards. The cadre applied the flaming torches to the placards and stepped back. The pile of still-soggy placards failed to ignite.

As the placard pyre fizzled, Ouane repeated his call to "BURN" out corruption. Two more cadre ran forward, applying torches to placard pyre, and this time a faint trickle of smoke curled in the air. The pyre, however, stubbornly refused to catch fire. One of the Filipino technicians suddenly ran forward carrying a gerry can of gasoline. He poured it over the placards as two more cadre rushed forward with their torches. Finally, a flicker of blue smoke curled up from the bottom of the pile, until the placards suddenly took fire. It was too late, however. By the time the placards caught fire and the pyre began to burn, the crowd had drifted away to watch a better show of couples copulating on the riverbank.

The caption of the Associated Press release read, "CUBS Rally Fizzles!"

The release added that "Corruption and Communism" had apparently emerged unscathed.

The Montagnards

Mountain dwellers are wild and proud, valley people soft and effeminate.
—GIOVANNI BOTERO, 1588

Dark-skinned, barefoot, and fierce, the mountain tribes, or montagnards, were not hard to distinguish from the lowland Cham. The men wore loincloths and strode proudly with a long-handled machete balanced on one shoulder and a crossbow or flintlock rifle on the other. The women wore colored blouses, heavy pleated skirts, and hammered-out silver necklaces.

Oudone referred to them as Peaux-rouges—redskins—when he pointed out the shadowy figures wandering through the marketplace during the day and melting back into the mountains after the sun went down.

When I mentioned organizing the montagnards as part of the nation-building program, Oudone, changed the subject. When I persisted, he told me I should contact Captain Pang Vao, a Meo and officer in the Cham army. Oudone said he would send a message to the district chief of Ban Ban, who could arrange for me to meet Pang Vao.

Oudone did not offer to go with me.

The Opium Trail

A Filipino Operation Brotherhood (OB) medical team was located in Ban Ban, and I asked Vitoy, a friend in OB, to go with me. Vitoy and I were the only passengers on the Veha Akhat flight to Xieng Khuong, the provincial capital and nearest airport to Ban Ban. Xieng Khuong was also at the crossroads of the poppy trade. The Veha Akhat flight to Xieng Khuong was known as "Opium One."

The Veha Akhat plane resembled one of those biplanes in an "Eddie Rickety-back" cartoon. Its floppy wings and two "half-engines" were wired to an oil-spattered canvas fuselage. The pilot was a wire-haired Algerian wearing sun-blotched khaki shorts and a wine-stained shirt with torn epaulets. He motioned for Vitoy to sit in the back of the plane on some rice sacks and for me to take the copilot's seat.

The pilot, Anton, turned the key, sending clouds of blue smoke belching from the engines. When the engines finally caught, the plane went lurching down the tarmac and lifted off about ten yards before the end of the runway. Once we leveled off, the pilot turned and told me to take the controls, shrugging off protests that I didn't know anything about flying an airplane. He reached over and took my hand, placed it on the control stick, and pointed to the compass: "Fly twenty degrees north." The pilot then dropped off to sleep.

For me it was an hour of bare-knuckles flying, trying to keep my eyes glued to the compass while maneuvering the stick back and forth to keep the plane on course. When a mountain loomed up ahead, I shook Anton, who woke just in time to nose the plane up into the clouds. When we broke out, the mountains were behind us, and a sprawling mustard-colored steppe stretched out below us. Huge prehistoric urn-shaped boulders, dolmens haphazardly strewn over the plateau, protruded through elephant grass like echoes of a pagan past.

La Plaine des Jarres (The Plain of Jars)

> The typical snow leopard has pale frosty eyes and a coat of pale misty gray, enormous paws and a short-faced heraldic head like a leopard of myth.
>
> —PETER MATHIESSEN, *The Snow Leopard*

Nosing down toward the airstrip, our plane hit an air pocket and almost pancaked when it landed on the dirt airstrip. Anton had to swerve around a water buffalo grazing on the airstrip but finally skidded to a stop at the end of the airstrip, across from the Snow Leopard Inn.

The inn, its mangy namesake tied to a banyan tree out back, sat aside the main junction of the "opium route." Over the years the inn has been a witness to a number of skirmishes and battles between the French and the Vietminh and has served as victualers to both.

Monsieur Bernard, the proprietor, reminded me of Casablanca's Sydney Greenstreet, except for Bernard's white safari jacket, which was caked with red dirt and wine splotches. Bernard walked out to the plane holding out a shot glass of pastis, the licorice-flavored French liqueur, for his old friend Anton. Then, noticing Anton's passengers, he went back for two more.

After another round of aperitifs, Bernard served us large bowls of bouillabaisse stew along with a bottle of Algerian red wine. When we had finished eating, Bernard joined us for a cognac pousse-café. I asked him about getting transportation to Ban Ban, and he pointed to two Cham soldiers who were stationed in Ban Ban sitting at another table. Bernard suggested that if I offered them a round of beer, they would probably be glad to drive me in their jeep to Ban Ban. I stood them to two rounds of "33" beer and, as Bernard had predicted, they agreed to drive us. Before leaving, I went over to Anton's table to say good-bye. I had taken a liking to the wizened Algerian pilot and told him I hoped to fly with him again.

I didn't know it at the time, but I would keep crossing paths with Anton many times as we plied our respective trades along the trail. The last time I saw him, we were standing again outside the Snow Leopard Inn. Behind us stood the aging biplane, which by then I had christened the Spirit of Xieng Khuong. The thud of mortar rounds could be heard off in the distance announcing the beginning of another battle for La Plaine. Anton clapped me on the shoulder. "*Plus ca change, mon ami.* Nothing changes. Another battle beginning that will change nothing. I hope *les emmerdeurs* don't hit the inn and spoil the best bouillabaisse in Southeast Asia! *Salut!*"

Ban Ban

The ride to Ban Ban was scary and gut wrenching. Spring rains made the road slippery, causing the jeep to slide along the edges of steep embankments and crash into thickets of vines and bamboo. The crankcase kept scraping over deep ruts, clogging the exhaust pipe and causing the engine to sputter and cough. At times the road disappeared entirely, the driver crashing blindly through the jungle until finally the road would reappear.

Sharp embankments offering ideal ambush sites loomed on either side as we drove deeper into the mountains. Bernard had told us after lunch about a convoy that had recently been ambushed by the Pathet Cham along this same road, which was probably the reason the two Cham had suddenly became silent, nervously scanning the ridges for a possible ambuscade.

Their fears were contagious. I felt butterflies in my stomach and began to sweat, even though it was getting colder the higher we went. And my unease was made worse knowing it was of my own making. I had been too nonchalant and blasé about the trip to Ban Ban, announcing cavalierly that I was "off to see the montagnards." I hadn't left an itinerary with the Station or bothered to have Oudone advise the local military commander we would be in the area. However, I was no longer feeling cavalier, bouncing along in a jeep and sitting behind two skittish Cham soldiers who had one carbine between them.

Even with the best of preparations, the case officer in the field often feels alone and vulnerable. His only companions are often only local counterparts or indigenous village chiefs and villagers on whom he has to rely for company and security. Unlike his military colleagues, the case officer has no backup, no cavalry or gunships standing by to come to his rescue.

Nevertheless, case officers thrive on their independence and freedom of action, on being able to use their initiative and operate on their own. He can take action and make decisions, knowing the Station will back him up. With that independence, however, comes loneliness and vulnerability, and riding deeper into the mountains, I began to feel both.

The butterflies and cold sweat disappeared when the jeep finally broke out onto a winding gravel road. A bullet-pocked concrete marker read ten kilometers to Ban Ban, and a half hour later the jeep pulled up in front of the Operation Brotherhood clinic.

The OB team greeted us with a warm welcome and invited us to stay with them. They prepared a barbecue that evening in our honor and invited the district chief. When he arrived, the wild boar was still turning on the spit. I introduced myself to Wang Si, who told me Colonel Oudone had sent a message about my visit. He invited me to call on him at his office in the morning.

The barbecue was followed by a Filipino songfest and dancing the *tinikling*, at which Wang Si was surprisingly adept, stepping effortlessly in and out of the clacking bamboo poles. I was not as agile as Wang Si, which my black and blue ankles attested to the next morning.

The district chief was waiting in his office when I arrived. Wang Si was a Black Thai, descendant of the tribal group that emigrated centuries earlier from the Black Thai river basin area in China. He was short, wide shouldered, and dark skinned, with a wrinkled forehead and squinting eyes. Wang Si's face brightened when I presented him with a "petit pistolet." He ran his hands over the barrel and then began pointing the pistol at various targets in his office. I was glad I had held back the box of cartridges.

Before talking to him about meeting Pang Vao, I asked Wang Si if he would be interested in an airport for Ban Ban. The idea had come to me as we drove into the town before arriving at the OB clinic. I didn't relish the idea of more jeep rides like the last one if it turned out I needed to make more trips to Ban Ban to meet with Pang Vao. I had seen a soccer field outside of town, a field that could serve as an airstrip for the Station's newly acquired helio.

The helio, or heliocourier, had been designed and developed in St. Louis, Missouri, by two airplane mechanics. Designed for short takeoff and landings (STOL), one of the first helios produced in St. Louis had been sent to Viensiang for use in our up-country operations. Ban Ban would be an ideal destination for its inaugural flight.

Wang Si jumped at the idea of an airport in Ban Ban. "*Magnifique!*" he declared.

When I suggested the soccer field as a possible site, Wang Si immediately agreed and said he would speak to the commander of the military outpost near the field. He would ask him to have his soldiers remove rocks and stumps along the sides and at either end of the proposed runway.

Having settled the question of the airport, I asked Wang Si if he could arrange for me to meet Captain Pang Vao. Wang Si replied that Pang Vao was "like his brother," and he would have no trouble arranging a meeting. He said he would immediately send a message asking Pang Vao to come to Ban Ban to meet me.

Wang Si hadn't asked why I wanted to see Pang Vao and didn't mention having to obtain the approval of the province chief or regional military commander, which would be normal in arranging a meeting between a Cham officer and a foreigner. It seemed that Wang Si ran his district with little outside interference, and I attributed this to the isolation of his district. In the case of Pang Vao, he pointed out that he was a "fellow montagnard."

I met Pang Vao three days later in Wang Si's office. The Meo captain was short, like Wang Si, but much thinner and wirier. Pang Vao had high cheekbones, slightly slanted eyes, and a ruddy complexion. Although he had been walking for two days to get to Ban Ban, he didn't seem tired. Pang Vao had a reservoir of restless energy and was constantly shifting back and forth on the balls of his feet as he talked.

After introducing me to Pang Vao, Wang Si left us alone in his office. I told the captain I had heard a lot about him. I had looked forward to meeting him so I could discuss a project with him concerning the montagnards. I was about to continue, but Pang Vao cut me off. Pang Vao's habit of interrupting was one I would have to get used to.

He said he had been waiting for a long time to meet someone from the American embassy. He wanted to discuss the current situation concerning his Meo, a situation that was grave, *tres tres* grave. We could discuss my project later.

Pang Vao spoke in rapid French for almost an hour. He began by berating the French. He said that after they lost the Indochina War, they disarmed the thousands of Meo they had recruited as maquis to fight the Vietminh and help the French control the highlands. Disarming the Meo, according to Pang Vao, was a big mistake, because taking a Meo's rifle is like taking his soul. A number of Meo had hidden their weapons from the French, but they were all still bitter about having been betrayed.

Pang Vao would keep coming back to the betrayal, which had deeply embittered him against the French.

Getting back to the "grave" situation, Pang Vao said the Meo desperately needed help. The Cham government didn't care about the tribal people and couldn't or wouldn't help them. The Cham had appointed a "token Meo" as minister of Montagnard affairs, but he became corrupted by Cham politicians and had done nothing to help his fellow montagnards.

Pang Vao said the Meo depended heavily on their opium crop, which they bartered for rice, blankets, and cooking oil. This year's opium crop had been almost wiped out by heavy rains along with having to suffer through a harsh winter. Also, Vietnamese marauders had been increasing their raids across the border to steal their livestock.

With another winter approaching, the Meo were becoming desperate. Pang Vao said his people needed my help.

The Meo leader had caught me off guard. My proposal for integrating his montagnards into a nation-building program would ring hollow. Pang Vao wanted tangible help for his people, who were in desperate straits. Offering civic action kits and community radio sets wasn't going to cut it. At the same time, I didn't want to raise false hopes with a man who had a strong memory of false promises. I had to come up with something.

I told Pang Vao how much I admired the Meo and could sympathize with their plight. Unfortunately, my agency's resources were limited. We didn't have magic fertilizers to revive the opium crop or hybrid seeds to start a new one. We couldn't feed the entire Meo population, and as for their depleting livestock, we couldn't provide arms for cross-border raids against North Vietnamese rustlers.

Pang Vao was obviously disappointed. His face fell but lit up when I said we might be able to offer some relief for his people. We could, for example, supply four or five tons of rice for Nong Het, several hundred blankets, and forty or fifty medical kits. We could also supply some carbines and pistols for his village chiefs, plus a community radio for Nong Het.

It didn't compare to Pang Vao's wish list, but the Meo leader was pleased with my offer and even asked me to repeat the list so he could take notes. When he finished jotting down the items I had mentioned, he looked up and smiled. Pang Vao said he knew we would help his people.

I wasn't off the hook, however. Pang Vao added that he had a "special request." He wanted *une enclume* for Nong Het.

I tried to think. *Une enclume?*

Seeing that I was puzzled, Pang Vao drew *une enclume* in the air. Horizontal and flat at one end, vertical and rounded at the other. It was about two feet high and very heavy. I finally got it. Pang Vao wanted an anvil. He explained that the Meo were skilled metal craftsmen, who made their own tools, flintlocks, and the famous Meo silver neckpieces. The only anvil in Nong Het had cracked and later broken in half. They desperately needed a new one.

I told Pang Vao we would try to get him an anvil, and before he could think of any other requests, I asked him to sit down at Wang Si's desk so we could work out a plan for an airdrop.

Pang Vao knew all about drop zones, smoke signals, and "Ts," so it didn't take long to draw up a plan. When we finished, we poured two glasses of sum-sum from the bottle on Wang Si's desk and toasted to the beginning of our relationship, a relationship that would one day lead to the White House.

The Helio

And when I go away from here, this will be the midpoint, to which everything ran, before, and *from* which everything will run.

—A. S. BYATT, *Possession*

Pang Vao went back to Nong Het, and Wang Si and I went to work on the airstrip for the helio. Soldiers behind teams of water buffalo rooted up trees and dragged off boulders. White lime was poured into the furrows dug along the sides of the runway and into the "Xs" at either end.

Using the OB radio, I sent a message requesting the helio. I advised our people in Viensiang that the Ban Ban airstrip was clearly marked and secure. A return message advised that the helio would arrive at noon on the following day.

The next morning a crowd of Cham villagers and montagnards gathered at the airstrip to await the arrival of the "big bird." An honor guard from the fort practiced marching up and down the field. Local merchants passed out rice cakes and bon-bons. Village elders followed with gourds of the local "white lightning." Wang Si, as official greeter, was wearing a coat and tie for the occasion.

The crowd became quiet when they heard the droning noise off in the distance. The droning became louder until finally a silhouette appeared over the horizon. When the silhouette was directly overhead, it took on the form of a big silver emu. The helio had arrived.

The plane circled, dropped down, and came in low above the airstrip past the red and white windsock. I saw the pilot peering through the window, trying to decide whether or not to try to land. He apparently decided against landing, because the helio suddenly nosed back up and circled over the town until it dove down again toward the airstrip, coming in just above the trees. The helio hit the strip as the wing flaps banged down and roared past where I was standing. I could just make out the contorted face of the pilot fighting to keep the skittish jackdaw from veering off the runway and then lost sight of the plane as it disappeared into a cloud of red dust and white lime powder.

When the cloud lifted, the "big bird" sat vibrating, with its landing gears straddling the white "X." If it had gone an additional ten feet, the helio would have plunged into the ravine. When the shaken pilot finally stepped down from the plane, two OB nurses ran out holding a "WELCOME TO THE LINDBERG OF BAN BAN!" banner. The village chief's wife draped a lei of frangipani around his neck, Wang Si toasted the "great aviator" with a glass of sum-sum, and the honor guard passed in review.

The crowd surged onto the field to get a better look at the big silver bird. The scene would have made those St. Louis mechanics proud.

When we left the next morning, a smaller crowd was there to see us off, along with a bleary-eyed Wang Si. We taxied down the airstrip and lifted off almost straight up. Once we had leveled off and were heading back to Viensang, "Lindberg" turned and wagged his finger at me. "STOL, short takeoff and landing. But from now on, not that short, OK?"

Five Thousand Sweaters and an Anvil

As time went by our need to fight for the ideal increased to an unquestioning possession, riding with spur and rein over our doubts.

—T. E. LAWRENCE, Seven Pillars of Wisdom

A grumbling Al Incolingo left for Bangkok with Pang Vao's request for an anvil. The following day he sent a message saying he couldn't find any "high quality" anvils in Bangkok and he would have to go to Singapore. He could be reached at the Raffles Hotel.

At the same time, an all-logistics message to all stations was sent requesting any surplus supplies of blankets. Okinawa came through with an unexpected dividend, having located a U.S. Army quartermaster warehouse stocked with a surplus of army blankets available in thousand blanket lots at a dollar per blanket. The same warehouse was having a "fire sale" on GI sweaters left over from the Korean War: five thousand sweaters for five hundred dollars.

Viensiang ordered the entire stock of blankets and sweaters plus four tons of triple-sacked rice and asked Okinawa to ship the supplies to Viensiang on the next available C-46. The message also requested authorization to use the C-46 for an airdrop into Nong Het.

Incolingo returned with a "high quality" anvil packed in oilskins attached to a red and white silk parachute. The blankets, sweaters, and rice arrived later in the week on a C-46 cargo plane.

The pilot was "Shower-Shoes" Wilson, who along with the late "Earthquake" Magoon, had gained fame as a CAT (China Air Transport, predecessor to the Agency's Air America) pilot, dropping supplies to the beleaguered French garrison at Dien Bien Phu. Dien Bien Phu was not that far from Nong Het, so Wilson knew the area. Spreading out his aerial topographic map, Wilson pointed to Nong Het. It sat on a mountaintop surrounded by sharp ridges and limestone escarpments.

Wilson ran his finger along the spiny "horn-toad" ridges. "Dropping into Nong Het will be a real 'sphincter test,'" he said. "The only way in is through the Tai Lap Pass. Winds funneling through that pass will toss the plane around like St. Vitus' Dance. And Nong Het won't be any picnic either. If your timing is off, the winds will carry that anvil and its parachute over into North Vietnam!"

Wilson said he intended to fly in low over the DZ, so we could "free-fall," with no parachutes, the bundles of sweaters, blankets, and triple-sacked rice. If any bundles broke open, it wouldn't matter, because sweaters and blankets were not fragile. As for the anvil, he would drop down to three hundred feet, just enough altitude to allow the parachute to open before hitting the ground, but not enough so it would drift into North Vietnam. Timing was everything.

I sent a message to Pang Vao to prepare for the airdrop.

Another case officer and I were the two "kickers" for the airdrop. We clambered in over the bundles as Wilson filed a phony flight plan for Bangkok in case there were Pathet Cham spies in the tower. Once we were airborne, Wilson altered course for Nong Het. An hour later we broke out of the clouds and Tai Lap Pass was dead ahead.

Wilson hadn't exaggerated. The minute we flew into the pass, winds began buffeting the plane. Wilson had to fight the controls to keep the wings from scraping the scabrous cliffs on either side. The whine of the engines was deafening when we entered the natural wind tunnel, and I had to cover my ears, already popping from the sharp change of altitude.

When we broke out of the pass, I went up to the cockpit to get a better view. The Annamite mountain chain running from North Vietnam down through Cham was below us. The area looked uninhabited until I spotted a clearing on a mountaintop. Once we got nearer the clearing, I could make out clusters of stilted huts: Nong Het.

Perched precariously on a steep promontory, Nong Het from the air looked like a toy village that had been lowered onto the mountain by a gigantic crane. Goats and sheep were grazing on patches of slash-and-burn stubble that backed up to terraced yellow poppy fields. In the middle of one of the patches was a white "T," marking the drop zone.

A white grenade had just been thrown out on the drop zone to indicate the wind direction and signal that the DZ was secure. The whorls of white smoke dancing around the DZ recalled Wilson's warning about the unpredictable wind currents in Nong Het.

On the first two passes, we kicked out the sweaters and blankets. Then we made additional passes for the fifty-kilogram sacks of rice. When we had shoved out the last sack of rice, we braced our feet against the door and looked out.

The drop zone was a sea of olive-drab bundles scattered over the field. Several had broken open, leaving sweaters dangling like scarecrows from nearby trees. One goat, with a blanket draped over it, looked like the midshipmen's mascot trotted out for the for the Army-Navy football game. Other goats and sheep grazed on the field unfazed by the bundles raining down around them.

Two blasts on Wilson's Model-T horn warned us to get the anvil ready, and when the green light slashed, we pushed the oilskin bundle out the door. As Wilson had predicted, the parachute opened just above the ground, but a sudden gust of wind lifted it back up, carrying it off toward North Vietnam. Then, just as suddenly, a downdraft collapsed the parachute, and the anvil careened down into the ravine. As the plane pulled up, we could see figures scrambling down to retrieve it.

Wilson made a final pass over the DZ to signal that the drop was over. Pang Vao stood on a pile of blankets, pointing to the oil-skin bundle brought back up from the ravine. He saluted, recognition of a commitment fulfilled.

Several days after the drop, Pang Vao sent a message asking me to come to Nong Het. He would send an escort to meet me in Ban Ban.

I flew into the new Ban Ban "airport" on the helio. The airstrip was already paying off. A lieutenant from Pang Vao's garrison, along with two Meo guides armed with flintlocks, were waiting outside Wang Si's office. After exchanging greetings with Wang Si, we left for Nong Het.

At first I had little trouble keeping up with my escort, but once we began to climb into the mountains, I began to flag. After several hours, we finally stopped. A toothless old Meo stood in the middle of the trail holding out a gourd of sum-sum. Following the example of the lieutenant, I crooked my elbow and drank. The potent Meo homebrew burned down through my esophagus, then hit my stomach with such a jolt it made my eyes water. The jolt did, however, revive me, and I was able to continue our trek into the mountains.

At dark we stopped in a Meo village. We were invited to stay with the chief and his extended family, including a dead uncle propped up in a corner of the hut with a rice bowl in his lap. I was told he would remain there until they finished hewing out his coffin.

I slept soundly over the pigs and chickens, and the latter's cackling awakened me in time to have a bowl of rice before setting off again. Around noon we emerged from the forest onto a rock ledge. The ledge overlooked a deep gorge with a river rushing along a series of white-water rapids. The view was spectacular, almost as spectacular as the monkey bridge spanning the gorge.

The monkey bridge was a long tress of plaited vines, anchored at either end by gnarled saplings rubbed bare by the straining sinews, which gave them the appearance of dislocated femurs. Two vine handrails completed the bridge's "V" silhouette.

My hope that there was another way around the gorge was dashed when I saw one of the guides step onto the bridge. He grabbed the handrails, steadied himself, and began lithely walking across the bridge as effortlessly as a Wallanda walking the tightrope. When he stepped off onto the other side, the second guide followed him making his way across the bridge as effortlessly as the first. Then it was my turn.

The winds had picked up, causing the bridge to sway. My feet were shaking as I grabbed the handrails, causing the bridge to sway and vibrate even more. I was sure it was going to turn upside down and drop me into the gorge, but suddenly the wind stopped gusting and I was able to put one foot in front of the other and make my way slowly across the bridge. I held so tightly onto the handrail that my palms were blistered by the time I stepped off onto the other side.

There were to be more monkey bridges along the way, but getting across them became easier each time, with the periodic infusions of sum-sum. On the third day, the trail began to widen, and we broke out onto a dirt road. Nong Het lay just ahead.

I looked down the road and saw that both sides were lined with Meo. Pang Vao had turned out the entire village to welcome us. The villagers were all ages and sizes; withered crones, grizzled patriarchs, warriors armed with cross bows, women with silver neckpieces, and papooses peeking over their shoulders. They all had one thing in common: they were all wearing olive-drab GI sweaters. Some had their sweaters on backwards, some had tied them around their waists. Ancien combatants stood proudly, with their medals pinned on next to toddlers with the sleeves of their sweaters touching the ground.

A young girl in Meo costume stepped out to drape a garland of yellow poppies around my neck as I continued walking toward the village. I turned to look over my shoulder and could see that the villagers had fallen in behind me, following the Langley pied piper. I wished the director and Henry could have been there. It was their show and I was taking the bows.

Pang Vao stood waiting under a red and white parachute canopy, next to a faded red carpet with a shiny anvil standing in the middle. After a welcoming speech, Pang Vao, the village chief, and I took our seats on a long wooden bench. A Meo shaman appeared and began chanting and sprinkling buffalo blood from his goatskin chalice over the anvil.

After the anvil had been blessed, the ceremonial drinking of "horns" began. Water was poured into large jars filled with fermented rice, jars from which long bamboo straws protruded. The honored guest was invited to drink the first "horn." When I had finished, water was poured from a buffalo horn into the jar to replenish the "horn" of wine that had just been drunk. The village chief then sat down, drank a horn, and passed the straw back to me.

It was my turn again, this time to drink a horn with Pang Vao. Then another horn with the clan chief, another with the blacksmith, and the village chief's wife, after which I began to lose count. I was so full of rice wine my eyes were watering and my stomach was turning. I would probably have keeled over and passed out if Pang Vao hadn't rescued me by taking me away for a tour of the village. At first I reeled unsteadily beside him, but the cold air soon revived me and I could walk straight and see better.

Nong Het was much as I remembered it from the air—clusters of stilted huts strung out along the stream running past the village, goats and sheep grazing on the slash-and-burn plots, and fields of yellow poppies backing up to the forest. It was an idyllic setting for a village so isolated—and so vulnerable.

The following day Pang Vao and I rode ponies out of Nong Het, taking a rocky trail that led father into the mountains. After little more than an hour, we came out on a mesa overlooking a deep valley. We dismounted and sat on the ledge looking over into North Vietnam.

Pang Vao told me his people were very thankful for the airdrop. With the sweaters and blankets and the rice, they would be able to get through the winter. There was, however, a serious security problem. Pathet Cham guerillas with Vietnamese advisers had begun to operate in the area around Nong Het. Local hunting parties had been ambushed and outlying villages raided, and although the Meo were good fighters and were not afraid, they were outgunned, their flint-locks and French fusils no match for the enemy's AK-47s. Pang Vao added that well-armed Meo could not only defend their villages but also drive out the Pathet Cham and North Vietnamese.

Pang Vao hadn't given up trying to persuade me to provide arms for his Meo. I reminded him I wasn't authorized to supply him with the weapons he needed. He nodded, but I knew he didn't believe me.

The Opium Poppy

During my last day in Nong Het, I watched a bullfight between an aging bull and a Meo matador. The makeshift arena was a stubble field that backed up to a tapestry of yellow opium poppies. Sitting there watching, I remembered a conversation I had had with the then chief of staff, General Ouane. Ouane told me that if we were really interested in winning over the montagnards, we should take a leaf from the French. Buy up the opium crop. Some they shipped to France for "medicinal purposes," and the rest they dumped into the South China Sea. For a million dollars a year, the French gained the loyalty of the montagnard chiefs and had no trouble recruiting their followers as maquis to operate in the highlands.

I cabled Ouane's recommendation to Headquarters, but there was no reply. I had to wait until I returned to Headquarters to learn why.

In Headquarters, I heard that the director had apparently thought Ouane's suggestion about buying up the opium had merit and raised it with the director of the Bureau of Narcotics. The latter became so apoplectic at the suggestion, the director changed the subject and dropped the matter.

In an ironic twist, a decade later, when the drug problem was endemic in the United States, the government embarked on a massive program to buy up the worldwide opium crop, a big portion of which came from Southeast Asia's "Golden Triangle" and Afghanistan. By that time, however, the price of opium had gone up a hundredfold, and there weren't any takers.

The next day I left Nong Het with the same guides who had escorted me earlier. Pang Vao, the village chief, and the tribal elders walked out with me to the path leading into the forest. Before saying good-bye, Pang Vao took me aside, reminding me "not to forget the guns." Pang Vao eventually got his guns, enough to arm the largest "clandestine army" in history.

Nation Building: The Collapse

> There is a point in everything beyond which it is dangerous to go, for once you do so, there can be no turning back.
> —FYODOR DOSTOYEVSKY, *Crime and Punishment*

Back in Viensiang, the specter of the Red Prince still haunted us. To exorcise his ghost, we recommended establishing a CUBS chapter in the capital of the prince's home province, Phong Saly.

A nervous province chief convoked the local populace. Oudone and one of our officers who knew the province chief flew to Phong Saly in the helio, which was loaded with civic-action kits, a flag, and pins for the new chapter. Before landing, the pilot circled over the airstrip and pointed to the provincial headquarters building where the Cham flag was flying upside down. Dropping down lower, the occupants of the helio could see that trenches had been dug across the airstrip, exposing bangalore torpedoes probably primed to explode when the plane landed.

Phong Saly was not in friendly hands, and the helio returned to Viensang and Phong Saly remained colored red on Henry's map.

The Election

You think that . . . you are the pursuer . . . that it is your part to woo, to persuade, to prevail, to overcome. Fool, it is you who are the pursued, the marked down quarry.
—GEORGE BERNARD SHAW, *Man and Superman*

Election day finally came, and we crossed our fingers. I sat in the back of the press center set up for the foreign correspondents monitoring the election. The first returns posted were from Phong Saly, the Red Prince's province and the one farthest from Viensiang. The posted results gave 8,535 votes for the government candidate, 140 for the Pathet Cham candidate.

The improbable results were so lopsided in favor of the government candidate that the correspondents assumed there was the usual "communications glitch." When the next returns came in from Sam Neua, another remote province and Pathet Cham stronghold, giving 4,302 votes to the government candidate and only 380 for the Pathet Cham, it was obvious there was more than a communications failure. The correspondents jumped up, shouting "fix" and "foul," but the board remained unchanged. There was so much commotion that no one noticed when I slipped out the back and ran over to Colonel Sipo's office.

Colonel Sipo, a half-caste Vietnamese, was disliked and feared by his military colleagues. He was an ambitious officer and had persuaded General Ouane to put him in charge of "election security," a job none of the other officers wanted. I was certain the lopsided returns were Sipo's doing.

When I burst into his office, Sipo was standing in front of his desk, smiling. Sipo recognized me at once and asked me how I liked the results. I told him they were a farce and I suspected he was behind it.

Sipo was nonplused. "I don't understand. Your CUBS candidates are winning, the Pathet Cham are losing. That's good, isn't it? *C'est bon, n'est-ce pas?*"

I angrily replied that because of the lopsided returns, the journalists were calling the election a fraud. Sipo didn't comment, changing the subject to ask me when I was born! The election was a shambles and here the security chief was calmly asking when I had been born. I was still furious with Sipo but knew it was no use trying to reason with the pigheaded colonel. I turned and went out the door, shouting over my shoulder as I left, "And if you must know, I was born on September 3, 1927."

The election center was in a state of bedlam when I returned. The clamor abated only briefly when the returns from Khamouane, another Pathet Cham stronghold, were posted and gave an unexpected 3,927 votes to the Pathet Cham candidate. "3 9 27." My birthday! Sipo was trying to make amends.

He couldn't go all the way however. The government candidate got 4,108 votes.

In the end, it did not matter, because it was too late. The correspondents had already filed their press releases describing "the death of democracy in Cham."

CHAPTER 7:
Cham Coup d'Etat

"We have done with hope and honour . . .
We are dropping down the ladder rung by rung!"
—RUDYARD KIPLING, *Gentlemen–Rankers*

O ur program was a shambles. Jude, the patron saint of lost causes, had ridden back into Cham. An angry young parachute captain had staged a coup d'etat in Viensiang and installed the neutralist Prince Souphanna as chief of state.

The Station was caught off guard. We had been so occupied with our own program that we had taken our eyes off the opposition, forgetting that our Soviet alter egos were not about to cede their Cham fiefdom to interlopers from Langley.

Since the time was not yet ripe for the Soviets to intervene openly, they had scouted around for an agent of influence to keep their hand in. They found one in Prince Souphanna through their unwitting access agent, a young parachute captain.

The coup was a victory for the anti-CUBS neutralists and spelled finis to our political action program. It was an ignominious end to a promising undertaking. The unforeseen climax left us stunned and frustrated, but we had no time for hand-wringing or recriminations. The first priority was damage control, getting rid of the evidence.

Printing presses had to be dismantled, foreign technicians spirited out of the country, thousands of CUBS pins melted down or dumped in the Mekong. The "four horsemen" were then summoned to the same office where Henry had fired them up for the great crusade that now lay in tatters.

Headquarters had decided that the four CUBS case officers should leave Cham immediately before they were declared personae non gratae by the new neutralist government. Henry said we were to leave with the "nonessential" embassy personnel who were also being evacuated. Henry tried to put a good face on our leaving, telling us it was a "temporary measure" and we would return to Cham once the situation stabilized.

We did eventually return to Cham, although not to Viensiang. Henry, however, was no longer there when we returned.

Evacuation #1

If thus thou vanishest, thou tell'st the world it is not worth leave-taking.
—W. SHAKESPEARE, *Antony and Cleopatra*

Evacuations are benchmarks in the case officer's family chronicle. In Bangkok, after the first evacuation, Laurie won a track meet, Kent's first tooth came through, Gray came down with the mumps, and Megan rode in the gymkana.

We were sad to be leaving Cham, the kingdom the world passed by. Memories of swimming with water buffalo in the Mekong, cheering on the Dutch honorary consul in the betcha (rickshaw) race, listening as the British ambassador tuned our piano, watching our offspring go off to school with their pet gibbons, leaving the mongooses in the yard to warn off cobras and constrictors. Most of all we would miss our Cham counterparts and families.

It was an ignoble departure. We left like caravans in the night, a convoy of trucks and jeeps loaded with wives and children, dogs, cats, diapers, and four dispirited case officers, "baci" strings still tied around their wrists by Cham friends and counterparts during wrenching farewell ceremonies.

Buses were waiting when we disembarked in Bangkok to drive us to the Erawan Hotel, at the time one of two large hotels in Bangkok. The maitre d'hotel was waiting out front to welcome us, buoyed by the unexpected increase in the hotel's occupancy rate, which had dropped recently because of fears about the situation in neighboring Cham.

We stayed in the Erawan for more than two months. When we finally left, the same maitre d'hotel was there to see us off, only by then he had had enough of the "refugees" who were not the preferred clientele for a grand hotel like the Erawan.

During our stay in Bangkok, the four case officers were ordered to check in daily with the station chief in Bangkok, who only grudgingly accepted our presence, resenting all the attention the smaller country next door was getting back at Headquarters.

Each day when we checked in, the reply was the same: "Nothing for the exiles."

By the end of the second month of diaper changing, escorting wives to the floating market and Jim Thompson's Thai silk shop, and visiting the Bangkok zoo, we became convinced that Headquarters had forgotten us.

Then a cable arrived, assigning a case officer named Jack as base chief in southern Cham, where the antineutralist General Novasan had set up his headquarters. A week later two other CUBS case officers got assignments, one to northern Thailand to run cross-border operations into Cham, and the other to work with Jack in southern Cham.

I was the last to be assigned. My orders were to set up a base in Luang Prabat in northern Cham. A radio operator was already en route to accompany me to the royal capital.

The "four horsemen" were no longer "nonessentials."

The Cham diaspora families remained in Bangkok. Joy and the four children moved into a bungalow with the families and pets of two other case officers. For transportation they relied on buses, tricycle samlors, or sampans. The children played along the klongs, ate Thai satay from passing carts, rode elephants, and attended the International School. Joy went to work for the *Bangkok World* and, like the other wives and their families, waited for visits from across the border in Cham.

Luang Prabat, 1960–1961

What if I fail of my purpose here?
It is but to keep the nerves at strain,
To dry one's eyes and laugh at a fall,
And, baffled, get up and begin again.
—ROBERT BROWNING, "The Life of a Love"

A rusted-out Dakota C-47 lay alongside the runway of the Luang Prabat airport, a reminder of the downdrafts and crosswinds that made landing in the royal capital a precarious venture. The terminal smelled of cooking oil from the charcoal braziers of would-be passengers waiting, sometimes for days, for the next flight out.

As a royal capital, Luang Prabat was scenic but without pretensions. The gabled-roofed hotel, with its fin de siècle lobby and high-ceilinged rooms, recaptured Luang Prabat's colonial past. Aging Citroens and Deux-Chevaux were parked dutifully on the side of the boulevard dictated by the *jours pairs* (even-numbered days) or *jours impairs* (odd-numbered day) signs, more reminders of the colonial era.

Tribesmen and Cham wandered around the marketplace and along the river that ran beside the capital. In the evening Luang Prabat's civil bureaucrats and Cham army officers gathered at the Cercle Sportif to *bavarder* (chat) and watch tennis matches between the province chief and the king's chamberlain.

Luang Prabat's main and only boulevard led from the town's center down to the royal palace. There an arch of frangipani framed the entrance to the outer garden, while inside the palace in the main anteroom, the late King Rama Sipavong sat embalmed in a large glass jar, his body kept erect by the golden spike driven down through the former king's spinal column. The king would remain seated erectly in the funeral jar until the perfect sandalwood tree had been found for his sarcophagus.

The Cercle Sportif at Luang Prabat.

The current king, Vang Sathana, was not too well-known, unlike the capital's other famous resident, the "Blind Bonze." The aging monk was highly revered, prophesying from his tottering pagoda on a hill outside the city. Following the fall of Dien Bien Phu in 1954, the victorious Vietminh army had marched into Cham, moving toward Luang Prabat. The population panicked and most of the resident Cham were about to flee the capital when they heard a pronouncement from the Blind Bonze. He prophesied that the Vietminh would not enter the royal capital, and as predicted, the column of Vietminh bivouacked outside its gates. Three days later the Vietminh turned around and marched back to Vietnam.

—⚉—

With the help of General Ouane, the former CUBS president who remained in Luang Prabat after the Kong Le coup, I was able to rent a small bungalow for our base. Lucky rigged an antenna on a shed in the back and set up his radio. I sent the first message, advising Headquarters and Viensiang that the Luang Prabat Base was open and operational.

The pace in the royal capital was slower than in Viensiang. Ex-French colonials and Cham sat around the bar in the Palace Hotel, nursing licorice pastises and playing the dice game *vingt-et-un*, "21."

In the late afternoon, the mayor, province chief, military commander, and town notables gathered at the Cercle Sportif to play bocce (*petanque*), watch tennis matches, and gossip (*bavarder*).

Le Cercle was an ideal recruiting ground. General Ouane introduced me to most of the regulars, and I was soon able to develop a network of informants, including the mayor, the military commander, and the king's tailor. The intelligence I gleaned from these informants, after sifting out gossip and hearsay, kept the Base fairly well informed on the situation in Luang Prabat and the surrounding areas.

The Pi

And in the air . . . there fly Things, Beings, Creatures, never seen by us but very potent in their wandering world.

—A. S. BYATT, *Possession*

I wasn't the only American in Luang Prabat. Frank Corrigan was the U.S. Information Service (USIS) representative, Dallas Voran directed the U.S. Agency for International Development (USAID) program, and Colonel Oliver Nelson and his "sheep-dipped" (undeclared) Special Forces team, ran the military assistance program. The ambassador referred to us as his "mini-Country Team" in the North.

"Operation Genie" was the brainchild of Corrigan. Although USIS was prohibited from engaging in covert activities, Frank wasn't bothered by bureaucratic constraints and liked to skirt these by playing spy. Operation Genie centered around the "Pi," the mystical spirits revered and feared by the Cham. The Pi were invisible but were believed to be omnipresent in clouds, rain, forests, and the breezes wafting over the rice paddies.

The author in Cham.

Frank's plan called for collecting all the bottles we could find in Luang Prabat. We would then stuff them with leaflets before air-dropping them over villages known to be under Pathet Cham control. On the way down, the bottles would sound like the Pi making a whistling noise. They would break open and scatter the leaflets when they hit the ground, illustrated leaflets urging the villagers to "break" from the Pathet Cham like the "imprisoned" Pi had done.

The proprietor of the Palace Hotel supplied us with all the bottles we needed. Since most Cham couldn't read, Frank drew caricatures of fang-toothed Pathet Cham, and Voran ran off the leaflets on his mimeograph machine. I requested a small plane from Viensiang to drop the leaflets.

When the plane arrived, we briefed the pilot, and at dusk, when the villagers would have returned from the rice fields, we took off. Once over a target village, the pilot would throttle back the engine and the plane would glide almost silently as we threw out the bottles. He would then gun the engine and fly on to the next village to repeat the operation.

We dropped bottles over twelve villages before returning to Luang Prabat. It was dark when we returned, but Colonel Nelson's team had set out flares on the airstrip to guide the pilot. We had jettisoned our entire supply of Pi bottles.

"Genie" was a one-shot operation, and its success was hard to gauge. We did get some feedback, however. An itinerant rice merchant told the province chief he had been stopped by a Pathet Cham patrol, which warned him that American planes were dropping poison gas in the area. Another source reported that a village chief had called for a goat sacrifice to appease the wounded Pi that had crashed through his roof.

Corrigan's enthusiasm for unorthodox operations like the Pi finally got him killed. He knew he couldn't keep calling on the Base for planes for his airdrops, so he chartered the only private plane in the area for a special leaflet drop. The plane was an aging Cessna, and the pilot had a history of bouts of delirium tremens. The plane crashed into a mountain north of Luang Prabat during the leaflet drop, and when we pulled Frank's body from the plane, he was still clutching a wad of leaflets.

To recruit and train paramilitary teams, I borrowed Colonel Nelson's interpreter, a native of the area with good Cham and montagnard contacts. Within six months, Luang Prabat Base had ten teams trained, armed, and ready.

Coordinating with the regional military commander, the teams operated primarily in the insecure districts east of Luang Prabat. A month after the teams had begun operating, reports came in that the teams were having some success in a district formerly controlled by the Pathet Cham despite harassment by the Pathet Cham. The teams had dug wells, set up dispensaries, and organized hamlet militia for village defense.

Reports from isolated areas tend to be exaggerated, and before reporting on the teams' successes, I decided to go to Muong La for an on-the-ground assessment of their effectiveness. Colonel Nelson volunteered to provide an army helicopter to fly us to the area where the teams were operating. The chopper dropped us off at Muong La, where we were met by the district chief. He had arranged for us to visit the hamlets where our teams were operating and, "for security reasons," to provide an escort to return at night to stay at his house in the district capital.

Nelson and I made the rounds of the hamlets, observing the teams digging wells, fixing roofs, and training militia. The villagers got along well with the teams but seemed uneasy about the presence of the two foreigners. When I mentioned this to the district chief, he replied that the villagers were afraid of Pathet Cham reprisals even though our teams might try to protect them. Late during the second night in Muong La, we were awakened by the thud of mortar rounds landing not far from the district chief's house. One of our team leaders rushed in and said we had to leave.

After a quick farewell to the district chief, we followed the team leader across the stream in the rear of the village, then into the forest. We spent the next two days hiking along jungle trails, giving wide berth to hamlets where our teams had been operating. We maintained radio silence, because Nelson's walkie-talkie could give away our location. At night we slept in groves of bamboo or in fields of rice sheaves, until on the third day we came out on a road that led to Luang Prabat.

When I arrived back at the base, Lucky greeted me casually as if I had just returned from a trip to town. I told him I was surprised he wasn't concerned about his base chief having been absent for three days. He said somewhat curtly he had assumed I had been "holed up somewhere with Colonel Nelson," and furthermore had not alerted Viensiang or Headquarters that I was missing, because I hadn't requested authorization to leave Luang Prabat.

It was one of many times that Lucky would cover for his base chief, and I thanked him for not sounding the alarm.

The Eclipse

Beyond the moon,
La lune ne garde aucune rancune.
—T. S. ELIOT

Doctor Henri, a French doctor, whom I had gotten to know fairly well, had come by the Base one evening to visit. The doctor had been in Luang Prabat for over twenty years, having stayed on after the French pulled out of Indochina. Dr. Henri was a fount of information on Luang Prabat personalities, most of whom he had treated at one time or another, and on local lore.

I had gone to fix him a drink when several explosions, not too far away, shook the bungalow. When I rushed outside, I saw tracers streaking across the sky accompanied by the sound of machine-gun and artillery fire ricocheting through the mountains. The increasing crescendo of firing reminded me of the "mad minute" demonstrations at Fort Benning, and I was convinced Luang Prabat was under attack.

I started to rush out to the radio shack when I felt the doctor grabbing my arm to restrain me. Pointing up at the sky, he said, "*Calme toi, mon ami! La grenouille est en train de manger la lune! Magnifique, n'est-ce pas?* Calm down. The frog is eating the moon. Magnificent, isn't it?"

Dr. Henri then explained that when an eclipse occurs and the moon blacks out, the Cham believe that the black shadow is that of a giant frog trying to eat the moon. The Cham fire at the moon to frighten the frog away, to keep it from devouring their moon. Once the eclipse is over and the moon reappears, it means the frog has been driven away, and then they start firing all over again to celebrate!

I looked up at the moon. The doctor was right. The shadow did resemble a frog.

I was still staring up at the moon when Colonel Nelson roared up in his jeep, jumped out, and asked if I knew what the firing was all about. When I explained, he burst out laughing. "I wonder how my logistics officer is going to explain to the Pentagon about a year's supply of ammunition having been expended to frighten off a frog!"

The Recoilless Rifle

Unhappy is the land that has no heroes.
—BERTHOLD BRECHT, *Life of Galileo*

Three Cham army outposts in the First Military Region had been overrun. The defenders, offering little resistance, had melted into the jungle at the thump of the first mortar round. Esprit de corps was sadly lacking in the recently nicknamed "Frightened First" Region. Morale was low. There was little will to fight.

Something, or someone, was needed to revive the Cham army's flagging spirit.

It was General Ouane's idea for me to go to Nam Bac. Captain Sang, commander of the outpost at Nam Bac, had been asking for reinforcements for his undermanned garrison. Since the First Region had no reinforcements available, Ouane asked me to go to Nam Bac and offer Sang some of our "special teams."

I told Ouane the special teams had not been trained to defend military outposts. They were mobile and only lightly armed, and their mission was psychological warfare and civic action, not static defense. If the teams were attacked, they
had been trained to disengage and melt into the jungle.

Ouane brushed aside my protests. He said the teams could be used to carry
out reconnaissance missions, to set up early warning networks, and to train
village militia, adding that their presence alone would boost the morale of the
understrength garrison. Turning on his best betel-nut smile, Ouane told me he
had already advised the commander at Nam Bac I was coming.

Nam Bac

The youth felt a flash of astonishment at the blue, pure sky and the sun
gleamings. . . . It was surprising that Nature had gone tranquilly on with
her golden process in the midst of devilment.
—STEPHEN CRANE, *The Red Badge of Courage*

The helio landed on the dirt airstrip and taxied to the end. A windsock flapped
listlessly alongside a corrugated iron shack. Several fifty-gallon fuel drums, probably
empty, stood next to the shack. The airstrip was deserted, and there was no sign
of Captain Sang. Johnson, the helio pilot, was uneasy. He recommended we go
back to Luang Prabat, but I told him the captain who was supposed to meet me
was probably out in one of the nearby hamlets and, having seen the plane circling,
would come down to meet me. I told Johnson to take off, reminding him to come
back the following afternoon to pick me up. Johnson shrugged his shoulders and
didn't try to argue. Once I was out of the helio, he spun the plane around and took
off, leaving me standing in the prop wash.

I watched the helio as it headed back to Luang Prabat and wondered if I had
made the right decision. The only sign of life was an emaciated cat, half-heartedly
chasing a gecko that had darted out from behind one of the oil drums. I looked
up the road that wound up the hill to the fort on top. Shimmering in the sun, it
reminded me of a French Foreign Legion outpost in Beau Geste. I was transfixed,
conjuring up ghosts of French legionnaires striding the ramparts in their white
kepis, and I almost didn't hear Captain Sang drive up in his jeep. Sang jumped
out and apologized for not having been at the airstrip to meet me. As I thought, he
had been out in one of the villages when he heard the plane fly over the fort.

Captain Sang was about my height, large boned and stocky. He had a mahogany complexion and, thinking back to the sun-baked fort, I was surprised his
face wasn't more lined and weather-beaten. We climbed in his jeep and drove
up to the fort. As we approached, a sentry called out, and the heavy gates swung

open. Inside the fort, fifty poilus in sun-bleached khakis snapped to attention and brought their bolt-action rifles to port arms. Behind them, on a raised wooden platform, sat two World War I machine guns and a 60-mm mortar, anachronisms in a time-warped outpost.

When we had finished inspecting his garrison, Sang led me over to his quarters, a room with a wooden table, two chairs, a bed, and a folding cot in the corner for his guest. Sang spread a map out on the table. He pointed to Nam Bac, which was at the end of the road from Luang Prabat, ninety kilometers to the east. Sang said Nam Bac was a rich rice-growing area, which made it a tempting target for the Pathet Cham. He suggested we climb onto the ramparts to get a better view of the area.

We climbed a ladder, its rungs worn smooth over the years by soles of French and Cham sentinels mounting to man their posts. Then we walked over to the northern rampart, which provided the best view of the town. Huts and kiosks lined the bank of the river that wound slowly through the town, then picked up speed to turn the rice-grinding waterwheels further down. The south rampart backed up to the forest, its trees almost touching the fort. It looked as if an enemy force would have no difficulty approaching the south side of the fort without being detected.

From the west rampart I could see jitneys and Citroen trucks being loaded with rice and charcoal for Luang Prabat and villages along the way. When the dry season ended, the road would become almost impassable, making it difficult if not impossible for transporting supplies, or the reinforcements, which would not be coming.

After climbing down from the ramparts, we got into Sang's jeep and drove out of the fort to make the rounds of nearby villages. The captain said he wanted to show me the area and he could also check on units of hamlet militia. Sang drove without an escort, because most of the people in the area were related to soldiers in the fort. He had recently noticed, however, that they no longer invited him into their homes, which he attributed to fear of retaliation from the Pathet Cham, whose patrols had recently been spotted in the forests nearby.

I could see what he meant when we approached one of the hamlets. The villagers were working in the rice paddies, and when they saw Sang's jeep approaching, the hamlet militia ran to retrieve their rifles, which they had hidden under sheaves of rice. When Sang lined up the militia to give them a pep talk, they were obviously nervous and kept looking over their shoulders. When we left, I saw the militia running back again to hide their rifles in case the Pathet Cham came by.

I asked Sang about the reports of Pathet Cham troops moving into the area, whether they were reliable or merely rumors. The Pathet Cham often used scare tactics, exaggerating the size of their forces before launching an attack. These tactics had been so effective that a number of garrisons had surrendered without a shot being fired.

Sang insisted the threat to Nam Bac was real. His reconnaissance patrols had spotted Pathet Cham units in the forests, and he believed it was only a matter of time before they attacked the fort itself.

It was almost dark when we got back to the fort. Sang lit a fire, and after a supper of rice and chicken soup, we pulled our chairs over to the fireplace. I decided to bring up the special teams before Sang asked. I told Sang that I had been reluctant to come to Nam Bac, because in spite of what General Ouane might have told him, our teams would be of little use in defending his outpost. Furthermore, if an attack on the fort was as imminent as he thought, our teams would not be able to get to Nam Bac in time. I added that I had reminded General Ouane that these special teams were small, mobile, and only lightly armed and would be little use defending an isolated outpost such as Sang's. I apologized for being so blunt, but I didn't want Sang to think I had come under false colors. The only reason I had come was because Ouane had insisted.

Sang nodded, poking at the embers of the fire that had almost gone out. He got up and added some more wood to the fire, then sat back down and turned his chair toward mine. He told me not to worry. His friend Ouane meant well, but Sang knew the offer of the special teams was a token gesture. When he had received Ouane's message that I was coming, however, he had agreed because my visit would give him the opportunity to discuss his plan to save Nam Bac. For his plan to succeed, he needed my help, which is why he was glad I had come.

Ever since coming to Nam Bac I had the feeling that Captain Sang was holding back. He talked about his understrength garrison, his shortage of weapons and ammunition, and increasing reports of Pathet Cham units massing near the fort. If Sang believed his command might soon suffer the fate of the Alamo, why was he so outwardly calm and unfazed? He acted like Captain Kurtz in Joseph Conrad's *Heart of Darkness*, not mad but borderline. And he had a plan to save Nam Bac. He went over and got his bayonet to make a sketch on the dirt floor. He scratched out a long tube with a sight on one hand, a trigger underneath, and a tripod to set it on.

"*Voila!* The 75-mm recoilless rifle!"

Sang was familiar with the weapon he had sketched in the dirt. At one time he had attended an orientation course at Fort Benning and had seen a live-fire demonstration of the 75-mm recoilless in action. He had been impressed watching the trajectory of white smoke as the rocket zoomed toward a tank a hundred meters away. All that was left after the rocket hit its target was a smoldering metal carapace.

"Getting back to Nam Bac. Let's say I have a 75-mm recoilless rifle and a supply of white phosphorous rockets. I set up the recoilless on the south rampart and aim it in the probable direction of the enemy attack. When the attack begins, I fire the recoilless. Whoosh! The 75-mm rocket streaks through the woods, leaving a trail of white phosphorous behind, slashing through trees and lopping off Pathet Cham heads! I fire another rocket, and another and then cease firing.

"At that moment, the loudspeaker on top of the fort begins to blare out curses from the Pi inside the fort, angry at being disturbed by heathen Pathet Cham who have no respect for the spirits. The Pi vow vengeance on the Pathet Cham unless they leave them in peace."

Sang was convinced that the combination of the fire-spitting weapon and the Pi's curse would panic the Pathet Cham. They would throw down their guns and run in spite of their Vietminh advisers trying to stop them. And they won't come back, because the Pathet Cham know Nam Bac is cursed by the Pi!

Sang looked at me and waited for my reaction. At first I didn't say anything, convinced that Sang had become delusional or was having a pipe dream. But when I looked at him, I realized he was deadly serious and tried to think of something to say besides how far-fetched his plan was. I was still pondering my response when I began to have second thoughts. Was his plan that far-fetched? Desperate situations call for desperate and unconventional solutions, and Sang's plan had elements of both. Plus Sang was convinced his plan would work.

I don't know whether it was the fire's reflection on Sang's face or a burst of sympathy on my part for the beleaguered commander. I thought again about his plan and that maybe it wasn't so far-fetched. He was probably right about the reaction of the Pathet Cham. They weren't hardened fighters like the Vietminh, and their awe and fear of the Pi was as deep-rooted as any Cham. The "smoke-and-fire" secret weapon and its disturbance of the slumbering Pi might tip the balance.

A quixotic Cham captain, a recoilless rifle, and the Pi. An unlikely combination that just might work.

I told Sang I would get him a recoilless.

The helio arrived the following afternoon to pick me up. Captain Sang drove me to the airstrip. I gave him my word I would try to get the recoilless and would let him know as soon as possible. After we took off, I asked the pilot to circle back over the fort. I looked down at the ramparts and over at the hamlets where the militia had hidden their rifles under the rice sheaves. I wondered how near the Pathet Cham were and how long Sang had before they attacked. Once we leveled off at three thousand feet, the fort and villages soon shrunk into small dots on the landscape. As we left Nam Bac further behind, I began to wonder if I had lost my perspective. The destiny of an outpost like Nam Bac, which had loomed so large in front of the fire, diminished as the dots faded from view.

I wondered what Headquarters' reaction would be to my request for a recoilless rifle to save some remote outpost that wasn't even on their maps. A fireside glow loses something in cable transmission, especially when the cable is laced with references to Pi and fire-spitting rocket launchers. They would probably pass the cable off as fantasy from a base chief "too long in the sun." I put my misgivings aside however and drafted a cable, which I had finished by the time we arrived back in Luang Prabat.

I handed the draft to Lucky, who took it out to the radio shack. He came back a minute later, holding the draft in his hand. "You really want to send this?"

I wasn't surprised at his reaction. Lucky was of that breed of radio operators who didn't hesitate questioning or holding back messages they thought were better "slept on." I had drafted several cables late at night, cables Lucky had found overemotional and didn't send. He would hand me the unsent cables the next morning and wait for my reaction in the light of day. I was always glad Lucky hadn't sent them.

This time, however, I didn't defer to Lucky and told him to send it as written. I knew it was the Pi that was bothering him, but I assured him that was what would get Headquarters' attention. In the cable I pointed out that increased enemy activity indicated that an attack on Nam Bac was imminent because of its importance as a rice-growing area and that its loss would provide the Pathet Cham with a plentiful supply of food and livestock. I then described Captain Sang, an imaginative and energetic Cham officer trained at Fort Benning. I pointed out that his garrison was understrength, low on ammunition, and with no prospect of resupply or reinforcements. I was going to add something about "stemming the tide" in northern Cham and that if Nam Bac fell, Luang Prabat would be next, but I scratched it out as overkill. But I left the rest in:

WHILE GARRISON VULNERABLE, SANG BELIEVES THAT WITH SURPRISE AND EXTRA FIREPOWER PROVIDED BY 75 MM RECOILLESS RIFLE, NAM BAC CAN BE HELD. PLAN CALLS FOR FIRING RECOILLESS IN DIRECTION OF ATTACKERS, ROCKETS CUTTING SMOKE TRAILS OF WHITE PHOSPHOROUS THROUGH FOREST SETTING FIRE TO UNDERGROWTH AND INFLICTING CASUALTIES ON PATHET CHAM. LOUDSPEAKER MOUNTED ON RAMPARTS OF FORT WILL THEN EMIT CURSES FROM "PI" SPIRITS AGAINST PATHET CHAM.

SANG'S FORCES WILL THEN RECOMMENCE FIRING RECOILLESS AND OTHER WEAPONS, THEN STOP AND BROADCAST ANOTHER WARNING FROM THE "PI" TO LEAVE NAM BAC. SANG IS CONVINCED COMBINATION OF FIRE FROM SMOKE-SPITTING "SECRET WEAPON" AND ANGRY CRIES FROM "PI" WILL FRIGHTEN OFF PATHET CHAM WHO WILL NOT RETURN BELIEVING NAM BAC IS "CURSED."

DEFENDING REMOTE OUTPOSTS NOT AGENCY MISSION BUT UNCONVENTIONAL WARFARE IS. CHAM ARMY DESPERATELY NEEDS A VICTORY AND HERO FIGURE WHICH NAM BACK AND SANG CAN PROVIDE. REQUEST ONE 75 MM RECOILLESS RIFLE AND WHITE PHOSPHOROUS AMMUNITION BE SENT LUANG PRABAT AS SOON AS POSSIBLE. WILL ALSO REQUIRE HELIO FOR ONWARD TRANSPORT OF RECOILLESS AND AMMUNITION TO NAM BAC.

The Agency is at its best dealing with crises. It thrives on nonconformity and doing the unprecedented. The request for a recoilless received top priority. Warehouses crammed like Fibber Magee's closet with Tibetan saddles and Russian uniforms were searched until an offshore support base came up with a recoilless and three cases of white phosphorous ammunition.

Ten hours later a C-47 landed in Luang Prabat with the recoilless and white phosphorus ammunition. The helio arrived the same day.

We had no trouble loading the case of white phosphorous rounds into the back of the helio, but fitting in the recoilless was difficult. We finally had to unbolt the copilot's seat, wedge the recoilless in kitty-corner, and rebolt the seat. I had to squeeze into the cockpit under the recoilless, letting it rest on my shoulder blade for the trip to Nam Bac.

The sky was clear until we climbed over the mountains, where we ran into heavy turbulence. Every time the helio hit an air pocket, the recoilless dug into my shoulder, leaving me with several black and blue souvenirs to remind me of the Nam Bac operation.

When the fort finally came into sight, Johnson throttled back and prepared to land. Then suddenly he nosed the helio back up, pointing to the flagpole on top of the fort. There was no flag flying and no movement inside the fort. I asked the pilot to buzz the fort and the villages nearby. Maybe Captain Sang hadn't received Ouane's message that I was bringing the recoilless. The pilot dropped down and buzzed the fort, and then skimmed over the villages. No sign of Captain Sang or his jeep, only a few sheep that raised their heads when we flew over. The normally crowded marketplace was deserted, strange for that time of day.

I began to have misgivings. Sang had agreed to fly the flag upside down as a danger signal, but not flying the flag at all didn't make sense. I thought Sang had probably been too busy preparing his defenses to worry about the flag.

I told Johnson to land.

The helio hit the airstrip hard because of the extra weight of the ammunition and almost lurched off the runway until the pilot got it under control and skidded to a stop next to the shack beside the empty oil drums. I wedged myself out of the cockpit and climbed down, putting chocks under the wheels, because

Johnson, the pilot, refused to shut off the engine. When I had descended from the plane, Johnson shoved the recoilless out the door. As I lifted it onto my shoulder, Johnson revved the motor of the helio and sent me sprawling on the tarmac.

I got up and looked around. No sign of Captain Sang, only an old man was sitting on one of the overturned fuel drums smoking a pipe. He seemed undisturbed by the vibrations of the helio engine, staring blankly at the figure standing in front of him next to the recoilless. I left the recoilless on the ground next to the shack and walked up the road to the fort. The sun was directly overhead, and I was drenched with sweat by the time I reached the gate of the fort.

The gate was open and I walked inside. The quadrangle where Sang's poilus had smartly snapped to port arms was deserted. Only a few withered tumbleweeds blew around the parade ground, and I had the eerie feeling I was being watched. I looked up at the parapet. No sentinels or legionnaires' ghosts, only a crow that might have been a vulture perched on one of the towers. I walked over to Sang's quarters. The door was open, ashes from the hearth blowing around the room. The bayonet Sang had used to sketch the recoilless lay in front of the fireplace. The chairs we sat in discussing Sang's plan for saving Nam Bac stood next to his desk. It appeared my Cham Davy Crocket and his entire garrison had abandoned the fort.

His great plan and fireside bravado had been smoke and mirrors, all for effect, for some reason I couldn't fathom. If it was all an act, as it now seemed with the dust blowing around his empty quarters, he was Cham's greatest thespian. On the other hand, maybe I was jumping too soon at the wrong conclusion and being too hard on Sang. And myself. Maybe after waiting several days, Sang had decided that the recoilless, like the promised reinforcements, would not be coming. Time was running out and he had decided to abandon the fort before it fell to the Pathet Cham and he had to surrender.

Time was running out. I could hear the thud of mortar rounds and small arms fire in the distance, no doubt a Pathet Cham welcoming committee on its way to Nam Bac. I decided I had better get to the helio before the pilot decided to take off and leave without me. I ran out of the fort and down the road. By the time I got to the airstrip, mortar rounds were dropping on the far end of the runway, kicking up clouds of red dirt. Johnson was waving frantically from the helio.

I ran until I reached the helio and started to climb in when I remembered the recoilless. It was still sitting on the ground where I had left it. There wasn't time to unbolt the seat and wedge the recoilless back into the helio. The Pathet Cham were already at the far end of the runway, but I didn't want to leave the recoilless for them to use in their next attack on another isolated outpost.

I looked around for something to disable the recoilless. I found a rusty iron bar near one of the oil drums and used it to pry off the sight and firing mechanism. I tossed them into the helio and then hefted the recoilless onto my shoulder.

I walked toward the old man, who was still sitting on one of the oil drums, unperturbed by the mortar rounds thudding along the runway. As I walked toward him, I could see that he was smiling, almost as if he was expecting me. He put his pipe down, braced himself against the fuel drum, and slowly managed to get to his feet. As he was pulling himself up, I noticed the faded patches on his khaki shirt where chevrons had once been sewn. He was *un ancien combatant*, a montagnard veteran who served as a corporal or sergeant in the French maquis.

The old man kept gripping the rim of the oil drum as I walked toward him. When I was several yards in front of him, he stood up straight, then brought his wizened hand up in a military salute. We stood there facing each other, the grizzled veteran and the young knight-errant. I lifted the recoilless from my shoulder and held it out to the old soldier, who looked puzzled when I tried handing it to him. He finally stepped close enough so I could roll the recoilless onto his veined, outstretched arms. When I was sure the recoilless was firmly cradled in his arms, I stepped back and saluted. "*Au nom du gouvernement des Etats-Unis, je vous presente ce souvenir en reconnaissance de votre courage et de votre heroisme. Je vous salue et vous souhaite bonne chance!* In the name of the government of the United States, I present you with this memento in recognition of your courage and heroism, and as a token of our friendship and esteem. Good luck!"

I turned around and jogged back to the helio. Johnson was pumping his fist out the window pointing to the mortar rounds "walking down" the airstrip. I swung up into the helio, and Johnson revved up the engine. We taxied at high speed down the airstrip around the newly cratered potholes. A mortar round landed fifty feet in front of the helio as Johnson pulled back on the stick, climbing almost straight up.

When we were high enough to be out of the range of small arms fire from the ground, I asked Johnson to circle back over Nam Bac. Pathet Cham were running down the airstrip and some had already reached the road to the fort. They apparently hadn't noticed the old man still standing with the recoilless cradled in his arms. As I was watching, he shifted the recoilless onto his right shoulder and headed into the mountains.

I still think about the grizzled old maquis and can picture him in his mountain hut above Nam Bac, sitting in front of the fire, watching the smoke curl up the olive-drab stovepipe, the metal plate at the bottom reading: "Property U.S. Army. Serial #168043."

The Funeral

The eleven-year search for the "perfect" sandalwood tree for the king's sarcophagus was over and a propitious date for the funeral chosen. The prime minister and his cabinet had arrived from Viensiang along with foreign dignitaries and ambassadors, including Averell Harriman, representing President John F. Kennedy. The ceremonies and rituals lasted for three days, culminating in a funeral procession of honored guests, each applying a torch to the funeral pyre.

Besides representing the president, Harriman had another mission. Following further incursions into Cham by the North Vietnamese, President Kennedy had gone on American television. Standing in front of a map of Asia, the president pointed to Cham and announced that here the United States was "drawing the line" against communist aggression in Southeast Asia. The Cham in Luang Prabat, including the group at Le Cercle, told me they were proud that the American president on television had singled out Cham.

The euphoria was short-lived. The "line" turned to sand, and Harriman was sent to Cham to work out an agreement with the other signatories to support a "neutral" Cham.

Colonel Nelson and I didn't know about Harriman's special mission when we escorted the former governor to the palace to have dinner with the king. We took advantage of the long walk to urge Harriman to put pressure on the Pentagon to send a battery of 105 howitzers to Luang Prabat for the defense of the capital and to back up Cham units elsewhere in the region.

Harriman nodded as we walked, which led us to believe he would support our request. Harriman's "nods" were deceptive. When we arrived at the palace gate, Harriman pointed to his hearing aid. He said he had deliberately turned it off because he knew we were going to ask him for support to the Cham army in the north. However, he had been sent to Cham by the president to negotiate a cease-fire, which he intended to do. He said he was sorry, but the defense of Luang Prabat was not on his agenda.

Harriman got his cease-fire, but it didn't hold, and the domino that was Cham tottered, then fell.

Guns for the Meo

A month after the king's funeral, I flew to La Plaine for a meeting with Colonel Kham Kong, commander of the Second Military Region. While waiting for the colonel to arrive, I was talking to Bernard, the proprietor of the Snow Leopard Inn, when Major Pang Vao rushed up. I hadn't seen him since my visit to Nong Het, and I congratulated him on his promotion.

Pang Vao was more agitated than usual. He told me Nong Het had fallen and his garrison and the villagers had fled into the mountains. They were now heading for a Meo area farther south.

Pang Vao pointed to the helio and asked if he could use it to try to locate the column from Nong Het. I agreed but said he would have to wait until the 105-mm howitzer was unloaded from the C-46 that had just landed. The howitzer had been flown in to help defend La Plaine against advancing neutralist forces. A U.S. Special Forces team was standing by to help the Cham artillerymen set up the 105.

A cable slipped as the howitzer was being lowered from the side door of the C-46, and the wheel of the 105 crashed into the side of the plane, leaving a gaping hole in the fuselage. A Special Forces team standing by rushed up to help right the howitzer and lower it to the ground.

Just as the Special Forces team managed to set up the 105, mortar rounds began dropping at the other end of the airfield. The Cham artillery unit immediately ran off, and the Special Forces disabled the 105 by placing an explosive charge in the breech to disable the howitzer before it fell into the hands of the Pathet Cham.

The C-46, a hole in its side, lifted off before the Plaine des Jarres changed hands again. Pang Vao and I ran to the waiting helio to look for his column.

We had just taken off when the helio pilot pointed to another C-46 off to the right. The plane was bringing in a second 105 howitzer and had lowered its gears on its final approach to the Plaine des Jarres.

Our helio pilot tried radioing the pilot of the C-46 to warn him off, but the plane continued its descent. The helio pilot continued trying to contact the rapidly descending C-46, with no success. He finally dove into the path of the C-46, forcing the bigger plane to bank sharply to avoid hitting the smaller plane. The C-46 pilot came on the air, cursing "the idiot" who had crossed into his flight path but apologized when he learned of the enemy "reception committee" waiting on the ground.

We then began searching for Pang Vao's column and eventually spotted it moving along a dirt road. Pang Vao asked if we could land on a clearing near the road, and we landed just as the column appeared around the bend. Pang Vao called out to the lieutenant leading the column who came over to greet his commander. I watched the column pass, a rag-tag mix of soldiers and villagers and two young boys in the rear prodding the sheep, goats, and two cows the Meo had managed to take with them from Nong Het.

Pang Vao ordered the lieutenant to halt the column and bivouac for the night, then asked me to come back the next day so we could talk.

We took off and flew down to Viensiang so I could brief Jorgy, Henry's replacement. Jorgy called for another officer, whom he introduced as Bill, to sit in on the briefing. I related the debacle of the 105s, the fall of the Plaine des Jarres, the search for Pang Vao's column, and the latter's request that I come back to meet him the following day. Following the briefing, Jorgy told me to return to Luang Prabat and wait for further instructions.

On the way back to Luang Prabat, we passed an Ilyushin cargo plane flying toward the Plaine des Jarres. The Cold War had come to Cham.

The next day Bill arrived with instructions from Viensiang that I was to take him to meet Pang Vao to discuss a paramilitary program. I knew Pang Vao was finally going to get his guns. On the way back down, we flew by an Ilyushin dropping supplies to the neutralists. This time the Russian crew waved to us as we passed.

We landed on the same clearing where Pang Vao was waiting. I introduced Bill, telling Pang Vao that he had come to discuss a "special program" with him. I then translated as Bill outlined a paramilitary program for arming and training the Meo. I noticed Pang Vao kept smiling and glancing over at me as he listened.

When Bill finished, Pang Vao turned to me and said he had only one question. "How can I be certain that your government will honor its commitment and not abandon the Meo like the French did?"

I told Pang Vao the U.S. government stood its commitment and would never abandon the Meo.

My answer seemed to satisfy him and he shook hands with Bill. Pang Vao then took me aside to ask me for a favor. Remembering the anvil, I braced myself. This time Pang Vao asked if we could transport his family to the area of his future base of operations. He wanted to be sure his family was safe, and he would follow on foot with the rest of the column.

I agreed, and once again, his request was not as simple as it sounded. It took the helio five round trips to transport Pang Vao's family of three wives and thirteen children to the new area.

Several weeks later I visited Pang Vao and Bill at the new base area. A Dornier plane was air-dropping rice, and several of the sacks hit Meo soldiers rushing out on the DZ before the drop was over. Following a buffalo sacrifice in their honor, I returned to Luang Prabat.

I didn't see Pang Vao again until ten years later, when I escorted him to the White House to present President Lyndon B. Johnson with a Meo flintlock.

CHAPTER 8:
Vietnam, 1962–66

The wrath of God lies sleeping. . . . Hell ain't half full. Hear me. Ye carry war of a madman's making into a foreign land, ye'll wake more than the dogs.

—CORMAC MCARTHY, *The Crossing*

There was still hope for Vietnam in the early '60s, before the My Lai massacre and Kent State made it America's tar baby. Vietnam was like its neighbor, Cham, having been ravaged by Mongolian hordes, invaded by Chinese warlords, and worked over by French colonials.

In 1962 Vietnam was recovering from the Indochina War, trying to grapple with a North-South split of the country dictated by another Geneva accord. The country was battle scarred, thousands of Catholic refugees were pouring into the South in another diaspora, while Ho Chi Minh and Ngo Dinh Diem solidified their control over war-weary rice-growing populations. Although Vietnam retained oriental charm, civil wars and the ravages of foreign occupiers had left pockmarks scarring its pristine beauty.

The years 1962 to 1966 spanned the prelude to the war, the landing of U.S. Marines, and the initial skirmishes in the "war of a madman's making."

Although my nation-building and counterinsurgency credentials had been singed in Cham, I was sent on to South Vietnam, where similar troubles were brewing. The assumption was I could apply the same poultices used in Cham to staunch the insurgency in South Vietnam.

Guidance to the Station from Headquarters contained familiar phrases about "strengthening the government's resolve" and "developing rice-roots democracy." There was a new one that had a good ring to it, however: "winning hearts and minds." Nation-building was struck and replaced by "pacification," civic action gave way to "counterterror" and "census-grievance," the Viet Cong (VC) superseded Pathet Cham as public enemy #1.

Saigon

Our house was on the outskirts of Saigon, across the river in Gia Dinh Province. It was a large stucco French colonial, larger than my grade and status warranted, but because of its insecure location outside Saigon's city limits, there were no other takers.

The house had a big yard surrounded with a wall covered with vines and frangipani. It came with a fifteen-foot boa constrictor that resided in a large cage with a palm tree in the center, a rock garden, and a small pond for the boa to bathe in. There were also two peacocks that were continually escaping over the wall but that were always brought back by local Vietnamese for the obligatory ransom of fifty rupiahs, or twenty cents.

We also acquired a young deer and christened it "Florence," then changed its name to "Lawrence" when certain appendages appeared. My trips up-country increased our menagerie. I brought back a small crocodile, a flying squirrel, and a two-foot-long boa constrictor, which I thought would be a good companion for the larger boa that came with the house.

I later gave the crocodile to the zoo after it almost snapped Megan's finger off. We kept the flying squirrel, which made its home in my study, flying across the room every time a visitor entered. The boys put the small boa in their mother's bed, setting off a small domestic crisis that was solved when it slithered over the wall to make its way to our German neighbor's house next door.

The boa constrictor that came with the house used the palm tree for his constricting. We named the boa Charles Willoughby, after the gluttonous G-2 on Douglas MacArthur's staff. Charles ate a live duck once a week, and his "feeding" attracted a number of foreign journalists, including Neil Sheehan, David Halberstam, Keyes Beech, and Jerry Schecter.

Every three months the boa shed his skin, and during this molting period, he would ignore the live duck offered him for his weekly dinner, allowing the duck to sit complacently on his head or strut up and down the scaly epidermis. After a week we let the duck out in the yard, where he would join the other "lucky ducks" spared earlier by Charles Willoughby.

—m—

I was initially sent to work with the montagards in the thirteen highland provinces. As in Cham, the mountain tribes controlled the highlands except for the provincial and district capitals and military outposts.

The Army of South Vietnam (ARVN) rarely ventured into montagnard areas except on "search and destroy" operations, brutal sweeping forays that didn't endear them to local tribes. So, to implement our Mountain Scout program, we worked directly with province and district chiefs, touching base with military commanders only when necessary.

My counterpart for the montagnard program was Colonel Hoai, a Vietnamese army officer who accompanied me on my trips to the highlands. Colonel Hoai's role was to act as my intermediary with province and district chiefs and report my activities to his headquarters in Saigon.

Hoai was an ideal counterpart. He rarely interfered with my activities, and because he was always hungry, he arranged most of my meetings with province and district chiefs before noon to ensure he would be offered lunch. After lunch, Hoai would doze off, which allowed me to work out the details of our program with the province or district chief. These officials were happy to support the Mountain Scout program. It provided them with paramilitary forces they could command directly, making them less dependent on ARVN military commanders to provide security for their province or district.

The backbone of the program, which I spent the better part of my first year in Vietnam implementing, consisted of twelve-man montagnard teams whose mission was to gather intelligence, harass the Viet Cong, and act as a government presence in the highlands. In provinces bordering North Vietnam, the teams were tasked to monitor infiltration of personnel and supplies destined for their comrades in the South.

I offered them a "package," which included financial aid and logistical support, including weapons, rations, and training. After the teams had been recruited and trained, I would make the rounds again with payrolls and supplies and try to monitor the effectiveness of the teams. Sometimes I would accompany them when they were operating in nearby villages, but my presence was a negative distraction, and I had to rely on reports from province and district chiefs.

A Mountain Scout training center was established in Pleiku in the central highlands. Bert, my former mentor at The Farm, became the director of the center, which received a number of commendations, including one from the president of South Vietnam for his course on animal husbandry and the prize pigs Bert raised for breeding throughout the highland.

A U.S. Special Forces team was assigned to the Station to work exclusively on the Mountain Scout program. The team set up a base in Kontum, the highland province where the Viet Cong were most active and from where they ran extensive infiltration operations into the South. The Special Forces unit trained our Mountain Scouts in hunter-killer operations and gathering intelligence on cross-border infiltrations.

Being in the center of a Viet Cong area, the Base was vulnerable. I was staying with the team one night when the Base was probed with small-arms fire. The team leader immediately lit a "flaming arrow" line of smudge pots on a pivoting platform. He then radioed for "Puff the Magic Dragon," the C-47 with a Gatling gun mounted in the door, which arrived overhead minutes later, spewing out thousands of tracer rounds per minute in the direction indicated by the flaming arrow. The tracers lit up the area in a Spielberg show of firepower and drove off the attackers, stopping any further probes for almost a month.

After eighteen months, there were almost two thousand Mountain Scouts on the rolls. I worked the thirteen provinces alone at first, then with two other case officers.

A program the size of the Mountain Scouts, however, was not without its problems. We uncovered a number of abuses and financial irregularities such as province and district chiefs using the teams to provide for their own security, padding the payroll with relatives, phony names, or even "dead souls." These abuses were not unlike those that plagued most programs in Vietnam.

My close ties with the montagnards got me in serious trouble with the Vietnamese commander for the highlands Second Military Region, General Vinh Loc. At one of the U.S. Special Forces' camps, montagnard tribesmen had massacred ten Vietnamese Special Force soldiers. Although our Mountain Scouts were not involved, Vinh Loc held me responsible and summoned me to his headquarters.

When I arrived, General Vinh Loc called me over and threw a set of photographs on the table in front of him, gruesome pictures of the mutilated and decapitated bodies of the massacred Vietnamese soldiers. He pointed to the photographs and started lacing into me. "This is what comes of your meddling with the montagnards and stirring them up against the Vietnamese!"

The general didn't mention the trouble that had been brewing for months, trouble stirred up by FULRO (the Force for Liberation Highlands), an intertribal organization agitating for independence. I was a more convenient target, and after another tirade about "interference in Vietnamese affairs," Vinh Loc said he was going to report me to General Maxwell Taylor, the American ambassador in Saigon.

He was true to his word. The next day I was summoned to the ambassador's office in Saigon along with General William Westmoreland, the American military commander.

I led off the briefing, beginning with a rebuttal of Vinh Loc's accusation that the Mountain Scouts were involved. Vinh Loc was venting his spleen for the massacre of his Vietnamese Special Force soldier. While no one condoned the massacre of Vietnamese troops, I said the ambassador should be aware the incident was indicative of growing hostility between the montagnards and the Vietnamese. I gave him a brief rundown on the activities of FULRO, pointing out that a rebellion was brewing in the highlands against the Vietnamese, and FULRO might soon declare independence.

The ambassador, a former four-star general and Westmoreland's commander in World War II, was visibly upset but directed most of his anger at Westy, whose Special Forces, claiming to have such close rapport with the montagnards, slept through a massacre in their own camp.

He then turned to me and said the last thing he needed in the middle of a war that was already hard enough to justify and explain was a "tribal rebellion," a war within a war. He then gave us our marching orders, which were to rein in FULRO and ask them to tamp down, at least for the time being, this call for independence, and to make sure there would be no more massacres in our Special Forces camps!

There were no more massacres, and the FULRO rebellion fizzled, but this was not of our doing. The war suddenly escalated in the highlands as North Vietnamese regulars began pouring into the highlands to engage South Vietnamese and American troops.

In late 1964 I was told to turn over the Mountain Scout program to the U.S. military command. With the United States now engaged in an all-out war in Vietnam, it was decided that large paramilitary programs such as the Mountain Scouts should be amalgamated into the overall military program for South Vietnam.

This decision taught me a lesson. Large and successful programs like the Mountain Scouts are tempting takeover targets. Keep your operations small.

Sister Rose

Please forget about the crusty scurf discoloring my sickly skin,
Pay no attention to my shriveled flesh.
                    —DANTE ALIGHIERI, *Purgatorio*, Canto XXIII

Although some of our operations in Vietnam were reruns of Cham, one was not. Sister Rose was a Vietnamese Roman Catholic nun who ran a leper colony near Zone D, a no-man's-land and primary Viet Cong base for operations in the South.

It wasn't clear why the Viet Cong had not overrun Sister Rose's colony. At one time the VC had captured Sister Rose and sent her off to a reeducation camp, but they sent her back when they discovered she had been organizing volleyball games between the guards and their prisoners.

Colonel Do Van Dien, the Vietnamese military commander of the area bordering Zone D, was a highly decorated officer and, like President Diem, he was also an ardent Roman Catholic and admirer of Sister Rose.

I had met Dien earlier when working with the Mountain Scouts. Two highland provinces were part of his military jurisdiction, and I often stayed with him when I was in his area. During one of my visits, Dien told me he was worried about Sister Rose's colony. Dien had received intelligence reports that the Viet Cong were planning to attack the leper colony, but he couldn't spare any troops to help defend it. He asked if I could offer Sister Rose some carbines and ammunition. It would be a token gesture but would bolster her colony's morale and maybe buy her some time.

Like all U.S. government organizations, the Agency is required to respect the constitutional separation of church and state. There were some rare exceptions, however, such as sharing intelligence with Israel and the Vatican, and I didn't think there would be objections to helping a genuine freedom fighter who happened to wear a nun's habit.

Colonel Dien provided an armed escort for my visit to Sister Rose. The gate was opened by a sentinel whose face was covered with pockmarks. Inside the compound, lepers with scaly skin and running sores walked or limped around the compound and, surprisingly, were all smiling, seemingly indifferent to their afflictions.

When I entered the compound, a bell in the chapel tower started ringing. Sister Rose was apparently staging an "alert" for my benefit. Lepers in various stages of the disease hobbled past to take up their positions on the colony's perimeter. Even those with only one arm or leg limped or crawled over to shallow foxholes, where they crouched or lay down, aiming their wooden rifles in the direction of Zone D. Women with flaking skin took up positions around a plywood mortar in the center of the compound. It had taken less than a minute for the colony to brace for an attack.

When the "all-clear" sounded, Sister Rose led me to the dispensary and poured out two glasses of "medicinal tea," which tasted suspiciously like Beefeaters gin. She told me about recent Viet Cong probes against her compound that had recently increased in both frequency and intensity, adding that the only reason they hadn't stormed the compound was out of fear of becoming infected. It was only a matter of time, however, before they mounted a major attack.

I told Sister Rose that Colonel Dien had asked me to help her. I said we could provide thirty M-2 carbines, one Browning automatic rifle (BAR), and ten cases of ammunition, not enough to hold off a sustained Viet Cong attack, but maybe enough to buy her some time and possibly raise the morale of the defenders. She thanked me in advance for any "donation" I could provide.

I returned a week later with the thirty carbines, the BAR, and the ammunition. Sister Rose blessed each weapon as it was removed from the crate and then gave me a blessing as well. She also hung a crucifix around my neck and called me "the Father Damien of Zone D," after the Belgian missionary who died ministering to the lepers on the Molokai colony in Hawaii.

I heard from Colonel Dien later that Sister Rose's colony had fended off several Viet Cong attacks before being overrun. She was taken prisoner and sent to another reeducation camp, probably one without a volleyball court.

Coup #2

On November 1, 1965, a cabal of Vietnamese generals led by Duong Van Minh, "Big Minh," staged a coup d'état against South Vietnam's President Diem. Air force planes strafed the presidential palace neutralizing forces loyal to Diem, forcing the president and his brother, Nhu, to flee to the Cholon district of Saigon. Shortly afterward, they decided to give themselves up, and General Minh, guaranteeing them safe conduct, sent an armored car to Cholon to escort the president and his brother to coup headquarters. When the armored car arrived, the bullet-riddled bodies of Diem and Nhu were inside, the two having been assassinated by the captain charged with bringing them back safely.

The day of the coup, air force planes flew over our house, diving and strafing the barracks of troops loyal to the president. I had gone into the embassy, but my family and the visiting wife of a CARE official took shelter under the stairs until the planes flew off and the bombardment stopped.

An hour later Joy phoned me at the embassy, telling me that the "special radio" was squawking and I should come home. The special radio had been installed in my house before the coup, with instructions that it was not to be touched except in an emergency. The radio was still squawking when I got home, so I picked up the hand receiver and immediately knew it was my friend, Colonel Lou Conein. He barked at me to "bring him some scotch whisky," and when I told him to get off the phone, he repeated his request, yelling at me to relay his message to the embassy. I learned later that "scotch whisky" was the signal indicating the coup was in progress.

I phoned the Station with Conein's message, and the acting chief of station told me to go immediately to coup headquarters, which was located in a military compound a little over a mile from my house. I was to tell Conein to contact the Station immediately.

I jumped in my jeep and drove out to coup headquarters, where the armored car with the bodies of Diem and Nhu had arrived. The entire press corps was standing around the armored car, and then several journalists began to leave the compound to file their stories. They were heading in the direction of my jeep, which I had parked near the gate of the compound. I jumped out, ducked down behind the jeep, and, using my radio, called my station chief in the embassy. I told him that I couldn't get to Conein without passing a phalanx of reporters.

Dave Smith, the acting chief, told me to forget Conein and get out of the compound, saying, "If those correspondents see you, it will confirm their suspicions that CIA is behind the coup. And you and I will be on the next plane home!"

I jumped in the jeep and got away without being observed. In the end my exit didn't make much difference, because the press accused the CIA anyway of being behind the coup.

The coup, which even the communist journalist Wilfred Burchett described as a "colossal American blunder," destabilized the country. A succession of "general's coups" followed the one against Diem, until finally Nguyen Van Thieu, the only general left standing, took over and became the last president of South Vietnam.

"Clear the Decks"

After the coup, the situation in Saigon remained tense. Our family's life went on, but not quite as before. Kent and Gray, wearing green berets and cut-down camouflage uniforms given them by a Special Forces "A Team" commander, played war games and built sandbag revetments in the yard. Laurie was at a movie when a Viet Cong terrorist lobbed a grenade into the theater. Laurie, having been told to lie on the floor in the event of a bomb explosion, did as instructed but was trampled by other moviegoers running out of the theater. The bombing left Laurie with permanent ear damage and recurring nightmares.

A Viet Cong car bomb exploded in front of the American embassy, killing a CIA secretary and leaving the CIA station chief, Peer de Silva, with permanent eye damage. On Christmas Eve the same year an explosion rocked the Rex Hotel, an American officers' billet, and with the security situation worsening, U.S. military police were assigned to ride shotgun on school buses and stand guard on the roof of the American School.

The situation in Saigon continued to deteriorate with a series of plastic explosive and grenade attacks, the self-immolation of Buddhist monks, civil unrest, and a rash of assassination attempts. A magazine photo of a South Vietnamese police colonel executing a blindfolded prisoner and the self-immolation of a Buddhist monk received wide play in the United States.

President Johnson decided it was time to "clear the decks."

Evacuation #2

Another evacuation. Cham déjà vu. Families were put on notice to be prepared for evacuation by military aircraft from Tan San Nhut airport. Joy and the wives of two other case officers who also didn't like flying wondered if they could be evacuated by ship. We looked around and learned that a Norwegian freighter was in port. The three of us went down to the port to the office of the shipping line, where we were told the ship's next port of call after leaving Saigon was Bangkok. We asked if the freighter could "evacuate" three American families.

The Norwegians were very helpful and relayed the request from "the American embassy" to assist in the evacuation of three families from Saigon. The company immediately authorized the ship to take the three families and their pets to Bangkok. Three days after leaving Saigon, the three families walked down the gangplank in Bangkok.

The second time around was easier. The families bypassed the Erawan this time and rented houses scattered around the city. Picking up where they had left off, Joy went back to work for the *Bangkok World*; Laurie, Kent, Gray, and Megan reenrolled in the international school; and they all resumed their riding lessons, eating off noodle carts, and hopping on three-wheeled samlors.

Bangkok was elevated to status as a "safe haven."

The Shrimp Soldiers

This is the kind of war that will wind on and make fools of its partners and opponents both.

—MARK HALPERIN, *A Soldier of the Great War*

Nguyen Van Buu was a Vietnamese businessman close to President Diem. He had the shrimp monopoly in Vung Tau on Vietnam's southern coast and his own paramilitary force to secure the road between Saigon and Vung Tau. He supported his three hundred armed, mobile, and very effective "shrimp soldiers" out of his own pocket.

I had gotten to know Buu after turning over the Mountain Scout program and had begun working in the southern part of Vietnam. Buu had a training site near Vung Tau, which he offered to let me use for our political action trainees. At the graduation ceremony for our first fifty trainees, Buu introduced me to his friend, Colonel Nguyen Van Thieu, commander of the Fifth ARVN Division, and later president of South Vietnam.

Because of Buu's close ties to President Diem, he was arrested after the coup against Diem. He would have been executed if his friend, Colonel Thieu, hadn't intervened. When Buu was sent to prison on Con Son Island, Thieu took over his mistress, Anna, a former Air Vietnam hostess. I last saw Buu when I visited him on the prison island. President Thieu was still looking out for his old friend Buu and at Anna's request arranged for me to go down and see him.

I was met at the airstrip by the governor of the island, who invited me to join him and "his friend," Buu, for a picnic on the beach. It was a tranquil setting for a prison island. We had our picnic near "shark's cove" with swarms of monkeys swinging through the trees. It was a perfect site for a future Treasure Island–style resort, with casinos and plush hotels designed to attract rich Chinese gamblers from the mainland, Vietnamese businessmen, and even some former case officers.

Buu was never pardoned. He died on Con San Island. Anna eventually emigrated to the United States.

Colonel Chau

Following the turnover of the Mountain Scouts, I was assigned to the rice-paddy delta of South Vietnam. Rufus Phillips, a former case officer in Cham and Vietnam and the new Agency for International Development (AID) director for rural development in South Vietnam, introduced me to Colonel Tran Ngoc Chau, the innovative province chief, whose model villages, census-grievance cadre, and provincial reconnaissance (or hunter-killer) teams were having some success in a rich rice-growing province that was also a prime target for the Viet Cong.

Chau's cadre worked in outlying hamlets building schools, digging wells, setting up dispensaries, and training self-defense militia. His census-grievance cadre counted heads and solicited complaints and grievances, which they would then bring to Chau for action. The teams, working primarily at the hamlet and village level, were unique in a country where authority traditionally trickled down from the top.

Chau's secret hunter-killer teams were trained to eliminate Viet Cong agents and political commissars in contested villages where the Viet Cong were active. These teams were unfairly associated with the interrogation teams of the controversial Phoenix program.

I worked with Chau for over a year, supporting and aiding him in augmenting his programs. I found traveling with Chau outside the provincial capital was risky, and the province chief barely escaped a number of ambushes set by the Viet Cong and their North Vietnamese advisers. Among the latter, as I would learn later, was one of Chau's blood relatives.

When I was staying with Chau, we had long talks about the war. Chau faulted the government in Saigon, which he believed was so obsessed with "search-and-destroy" operations and the "strategic hamlet" program that it had lost touch with the people at the rice-roots level. His views, which he expressed openly, did not endear him to government leaders in Saigon, including the president.

One night Chau told me he was in contact with a North Vietnamese Army (NVA) officer whom he didn't identify. The NVA officer said he wanted to open a dialogue with the American embassy about ending the war.

Many South Vietnamese had Viet Cong and North Vietnamese relatives, but I was surprised to learn that Chau's "contact" was an NVA officer. I encouraged Chau to maintain contact with the NVA officer, and when I returned to Saigon, I reported our conversation about Chau's NVA contact.

The last time I stayed with Chau before returning to the United States, he confided to me that the NVA officer was a relative he hadn't seen in more than fifteen years and was surprised when he had turned up at his office. I tried to press Chau on the identity of this relative, but he changed the subject. On returning to Saigon I again reported Chau mentioning his contact with an NVA officer whom he had identified as a close relative. I learned later that the relative was his brother.

After I returned to the United States, I learned that Colonel Chau had been arrested as a North Vietnamese spy. He was charged with passing information to his brother, NVA Colonel Trong Hien. The arrest of Chau, who had become a close friend of his American military adviser, Colonel Vann, and had been extolled in the American press, caused an outcry in Congress. My son, Kent, who was attending Lenox School in the Berkshires, wrote me, enclosing a *New York Times* article about the trial of Chau. According to the article, during the trial Colonel Chau continually maintained he was not a spy and had "kept the Americans informed of his contact with his NVA brother." He named CIA officer Stuart Methven as one of the Americans.

My son added a tongue-in-cheek comment about having to learn from the *New York Times* that his father worked for the CIA.

Chau was sentenced to twenty years in prison, but in 1974 Thieu commuted his sentence and allowed him to return to Saigon. When Saigon fell, Chau was again arrested, this time by the North Vietnamese, who sent him to a reeducation camp, where he probably would have been executed if it hadn't been for his brother. After over a year in a reeducation camp, Chau was again allowed to return to Saigon but was kept under house arrest. He and his family later escaped from Vietnam on a fishing boat that almost sank before reaching the coast of Malaya. Chau spent the next year in various refugee camps until immigrating to the United States, where he and his family now live. We still speak by phone from time to time.

The Sacred Mountain

The Holy See was at Tamyin. A Pope and female cardinals. Prophecy
by planchette. Saint Victor Hugo. Christ and Buddha looking down
from the roof of the Cathedral on a Walt Disney fantasia of the East.
                              —GRAHAM GREENE, *The Quiet American*

In the apse of the Cao Dai cathedral in Tay Ninh, sixty miles from Saigon, the
"pope" pontificates from a cobra-sculpted dais. Founded in 1919 by mystic Ngo
Van Chieu, the Cao Dai sect at one time had more than three hundred thousand
adherents. Its panoply of saints included Jesus, Buddha, Muhammad, George
Washington, and Joan of Arc. To communicate with the spirits, Cao Dai elders
sit around a long Ouija board, which would emit vibrating messages from their
departed ancestors.

The terrain of Tay Ninh Province is flat, except for the for the cone-shaped
"Black Virgin" mountain in the northeast corner. The mountain, with a golden
pagoda on its summit, is sacred to the Cao Dai.

The Viet Cong in the early 1960s had occupied the Black Virgin Mountain,
driven the Cao Dai priests from the pagoda, and raised the Viet Cong flag. The
sight of the yellow-star flag flying on their sacred mountain was an irritant to the
Cao Dai, particularly the Cao Dai province chief, General Tat. I had met General
Tat several times, when he invariably asked for help in recapturing the sacred
mountain. He made the same request to Major Johnson, the Tay Ninh military
adviser. In the end we decided that recapturing the sacred mountain was justifi-
able. Recapturing sacred mountains was not an Agency priority, but an operation
targeted against a Viet Cong base was.

Together with Major Johnson, we came up with a plan calling for arming and
training two fifty-man platoons of Cao Dai commandos, the Station to provide
arms, ammunition, logistics, and finances and Major Johnson's team to train the
teams in commando operations. General Tat would be in command.

As a covert operation, retaking the Black Virgin Mountain was to be a "one
shot deal." General Tat recruited the teams, and when Major Johnson said the
commandos were combat ready, General Tat convened the Cao Dai elders, who
consulted their "board" for the most auspicious day for the attack.

At dawn on the chosen day, the commandos moved out. They climbed up the
mountain, skirmished briefly with surprised Viet Cong defenders, and by mid-
afternoon the "cult soldiers" had retaken the Black Virgin Mountain.

General Tat made a speech invoking the Cao Dai spirits and extolling the
brave deeds of the commandos. The victors then raised the ten-by-fifteen-foot
flag of South Vietnam, which had been handwoven by Cao Dai widows. But the
flag was so large it still touched the ground when raised to the top of the flagpole.

Finally, the wind caught the flag and unfurled it. It could be seen all over the plain and flew on top of the mountain until the fall of Saigon and the occupation of Tay Ninh by North Vietnamese troops.

The North Vietnamese recaptured the mountain and ran up a flag with a yellow star in the center. General Tat was captured and sent to a reeducation camp. His brother, who escaped and now lives in the United States, told me Tat would never be allowed to leave Vietnam.

The Cao Dai cathedral was gutted but is still standing.

Farewell to Arms

I had been in Vietnam for four years. Our counterinsurgency operations had given way to a full-time war. Census-grievance cadres had been disbanded, and counterterror teams had been sent back to their villages. Political action teams (PATs) had been incorporated into a National Pacification Program.

The Station had grown like topsy. Case officers reported to regional chiefs in a bureaucratic jumble that encouraged coordination and discouraged initiative. When I was told I had to get a ticket to fly an Air America heliocourier, I knew it was time to leave. Headquarters agreed and gave me a sabbatical.

Sabbatical

There was too much farce mixed up with the tragedy.
—ROBERT GRAVES

Boston in 1967 reverberated with echoes of the maelstrom I had just left. Flag burnings and antiwar demonstrations rocked the MIT campus, where I was enrolled as a graduate student at the Center for International Studies. I had persuaded my superiors to forgo sending me to one of the War Colleges, because "I didn't want to study war no more." Thanks to Henry Kissinger, whom I had escorted around the highlands and who put in a good word for me, I was one of first operations officers to be sent to attend a private university for his midcareer sabbatical.

The head of the Political Science Department at MIT's School of International Studies and one other professor were the only faculty members aware of my Agency affiliation. A recent *Ramparts* magazine exposé of alleged CIA infiltration of college campuses had become a cause célèbre, and I was warned to keep my head down.

The clamor against the war made it hard to study. I found myself tagging along behind draft card burners and antiwar protestors to "get a feel" for the mood of the country I had been away from for the better part of twelve years. I audited "sit-ins" and "love-ins" on the Boston Common and let my hair grow long. I wrote my thesis on parapolitics and pacification and was invited to join Kissinger's private "round table" on Vietnam. At one point we briefed presidential candidate George Romney, who later said he had been "brainwashed" on the war in Vietnam. Fortunately, his "brainwashing" did not occur at our round table in Cambridge, or I would have been called on the carpet in Langley.

A Thai graduate student and friend who knew I had been in Vietnam asked me to give a talk to his Harvard club about the war. I was reluctant to accept his invitation, because the week before violent student demonstrations at Harvard had prevented Defense Secretary Robert McNamara from speaking and forced him to leave. My Thai friend assured me I would be speaking only informally, and, besides, it was the students, not the administration, who had invited me.

I was having a glass of sherry when a group of demonstrators stormed into the club. I decided I had better leave, but my student hosts stepped in front of the demonstrators and talked to them, pointing out that I was their guest. They were welcome to stay and listen, or they could leave. Most of them stayed.

I didn't waste time trying to justify the war. I told the students I had spent a lot of time in Vietnam attending funerals of schoolteachers, nurses, and hamlet officials assassinated by the Viet Cong. Contrary to popular belief, I said the Viet Cong were not the shining freedom fighters portrayed in the media. To the contrary, they had no compunction about beheading innocent villagers and sticking their heads in toilet bowls. The insurgency was not a "people's revolution," and brutal acts had been committed by both sides. The people of South Vietnam wanted only to live in peace and tend to their rice paddies, and even though they might have little use for their own government, they didn't want to be dominated by the North Vietnamese.

When the talk was over, I was surprised both by the applause and by later comments that this was the first time they had heard about the atrocities committed by the other side. In the end, I learned more from them than they did from me. They told me their biggest problem with the war was that the government and the Pentagon kept lying about it with their constant barrage of propaganda saying that we were "winning hearts and minds," that we were fighting for a just cause, and that there was a "light at the end of the tunnel." One student told me something that kept coming back to me as the antiwar protests reached a crescendo. "Our government lies at its peril."

My sabbatical went fast. In June 1967, I donned cap and gown. My family came down from New Hampshire and applauded when I was handed my master's degree in international relations.

I said good-bye to my hippie classmates, had my hair cut, and went back to Langley, where I learned of my new assignment: Deputy Chief, Samudra.

CHAPTER 9: **Samudra**

Espionage . . . the most contagious plague of courts . . . a viper among
roses . . . spider of antechambers weaving the strands of its subtle talk
to catch every passing fly, parrot with curved beak reporting everything
it hears. . . . All qualities of which anyone would be ashamed, save the
one . . . born to the service of evil.

—UMBERTO ECO, *The Island of the Day Before*

The Samudran archipelago, more than three thousand islands covering an area of 750 square miles, is known for its volcanoes, java coffee, Melanese dancers, batik cloth, and fire-spitting dragons. Rich in oil, spices, and minerals, the country's revenues pile up, ensuring that the mainland and outer island Samudrans could maintain their laid-back tropical lifestyle.

Following World War II, Samudra gained its independence from colonial rule, and Bwang Karno became its first president. During the Cold War, the neutralist president sided with the Soviet Union, which showed its appreciation by equipping and training the Samudran armed forces presenting the navy with two frigates and a battle cruiser and equipping the air force with a squadron of MiGs.

Alarmed about the country's list toward the Soviet Union, a group of army officers decided to act. The cabal overthrew the leftist president, stuffed the bodies of his pro-communist generals in a crocodile hole, and proclaimed the cabal's leader, Colonel Suwanto, president.

———

I arrived in Bintang, the Samudran capital, in 1969. My first task, as deputy chief of station (DCOS), was to coordinate with the Samudrans plans for the coming visit of President Richard Nixon. The mayor of Bintang had taken pains to spruce up the capital for the visit, including painting one side of the navy's one battle cruiser, a gift from the USSR, that would be visible to the presidential motorcade.

Joy, Gray, and Megan arrived a month after the visit. Laurie, having graduated from Langley High School, had married the son of an Agency officer and moved to Charlottesville, Virginia. Since there was no high school in Bintang, Kent was sent to boarding school in the Berkshires. A year after his graduation from Jakanda's International School, Gray left to attend Australia's Geelong School, which sent students for a year to "Timbertop" in the Australian highlands, where, in addition to their studies, the students underwent a toughening process previously undergone by Prince Charles, heir to the British throne.

During the summer, Bill Bell, director of the International Nickel Company for Southeast Asia, arranged temporary jobs for the boys on a volcanic nickel-rich island off the Samudran coast, where they learned the basics of surveying, mining, and prospecting.

Laurie came one fall with Marcus, our first grandchild.

The Russians

President Suwanto, even though a hard-line anticommunist, hadn't gotten around to expelling the large contingent of Soviet "advisers" left over from the precoup era. Bintang, with so many Russians around, was a beehive of espionage activity and ideal hunting ground for Soviet stalkers.

Recruiting Russians had always been the province of the Soviet Division, which held that only its officers had the sophistication necessary to run operations against the Soviet target. The recruiting record of the Soviet Division had been so dismal, however, that the task of recruiting Russians had been turned over to the field.

The Soviet official is a hard nut to crack. The case officer pursuing his Russian quarry has to start from scratch, because of the paucity of case studies to draw on. Most of the Soviet Division's agents were "walk-ins" who had knocked on the doors of American embassies asking for asylum and a free trip to the U.S.A. Case studies of the few "moles" not interred in the Siberian steppes or those still mining the lodes of the Kremlin were kept under lock and key in the tombs of the Soviet Division.

Defector files were available, but since most defectors are suspect agent provocateurs or "doubles" run by the Soviet intelligence service, the KGB (Committee for State Security), counterintelligence officers, responsible for ferreting out moles and penetrations of the Agency, are anathema to case officers who look upon them as vultures ready to descend and expose the cancerous insides of their recruited agents.

Nevertheless, recruitment of Soviets was the biggest game in most Stations of any size, and Bintang, with its large Soviet presence, was a privileged spy game preserve, abounding with spoor for hunting these priority targets.

The Soviets in Samudra, although numerous, were hard to get at. Most lived in the Soviet compound, but a few KGB and GRU (Soviet Military Intelligence) "trusties" were allowed to live outside the compound in Bintang.

Once the case officer selected his target, he would run name checks for background information, which was usually not very informative: heavy drinker (most Soviets living abroad), woman chaser (with their wives in Moscow, almost all were philanderers), hard-line communist (he wouldn't have been allowed outside the USSR if he weren't).

Contacting Soviets was difficult, and the case officer had to use his ingenuity. Surveillance was difficult, because pale-faced case officers didn't blend in with dark-skinned Samudrans. Vehicular surveillance was possible, however. Cars belonging to foreign embassies were identifiable by their CD (diplomatic corps) license plates, with each country being assigned a numerical prefix. CD-37 was the Soviet embassy prefix, and one case officer deliberately smashed into a CD-37 car as it left the Soviet compound, assuming the Soviet would get out of his car to inspect the damage, allowing the case officer, after exchanging insurance information, to try to arrange for a future meeting.

This particular Soviet, however, did not get out of his car, leaving his chauffer to inspect the damage. The driver glared briefly at the case officer, then got back in and drove away.

Another case officer set his fishing pole downstream from where he had heard his target went fishing. When the Soviet target arrived, he spotted the interloper even though he was fifty yards downstream, picked up his tackle, and left.

To assist his case officers in contacting their Soviet targets, the COS asked the American ambassador to challenge his Soviet counterpart to an intramural volleyball match. The Soviet ambassador immediately accepted the challenge and fielded a team of burly KGB officers.

The semipro Soviets trounced their amateur American counterparts, wolfed down the hamburgers and the beer offered by the U.S. ambassador, and left before Station officers had a chance to exchange calling cards.

Yuri

My first Soviet target in Jakanda was the deputy chief of the KGB contingent there. Yuri was a known hard-core Soviet, and it would be difficult, if not impossible, to recruit him.

Yuri was short, arrogant, and crass, constantly hitching up his trousers and leaving his fly open. His suits were rarely pressed, and his gruff manner and rudeness hinted at this peasant background. He was my target, however, and I had to pursue him.

Yuri lived in the Soviet embassy compound. Since I had access to him only at official embassy functions, I decided use my daughter. One of Megan's friends had a pony cart, which the girls had recently been riding around in selling Girl Scout cookies to members of the international community. I asked Megan to make a detour with the pony cart and deliver two boxes of cookies to Yuri's apartment.

The girls, excited about their mission to the compound, trotted off. When they arrived at the gate to the embassy compound, they waited until an embassy car arrived and the guard opened the gate. They trotted in behind the car and were inside the compound before the guard could close the gate. The girls waved to the guard and trotted off to Yuri's apartment building, which I had shown them on a map of the compound, hopped out, and left the surrey parked outside.

They walked up to the second floor and knocked on the door of Yuri's apartment. A burly woman with a red kerchief tied around her head peered out, looking up and down the corridor. When she saw the two figures in green uniforms, she stepped back to close the door. Several other ladies, however, apparently visiting Mrs. Yuri, peered out into the hall and, seeing the girls, urged Mrs. Yuri to invite them inside.

Once inside, the girls opened one of the boxes and began passing it around. The ladies chattered and giggled as they sampled the cookies, until suddenly there was a loud banging on the door. A burly Russian burst into the room and began shouting at the women, pointing at the two girls. The women, however, were not intimidated and formed a protective circle around their visitors, shouting at the intruder, who was still pointing excitedly at the green-uniformed figures. It was a standoff until a uniformed Soviet entered and called over Madame Yuri.

The girls decided it was a good time to leave. They curtsied politely to the ladies, handed both boxes to Yuri's wife, and dashed out past the two men standing by the door. They ran down the corridor and the stairs and out to the pony cart, which was still standing by the curb. A crowd had gathered around the cart, and the girls had to push through them to get to it. Taking up the reins, they rode off, waving to the crowd of onlookers. When they got to the gate at the entrance to the compound, they urged the pony forward and ducked under the barrier before the guard could react. Once safely out of the compound, they turned and waved to the guard, who was shaking his fist in the air.

The girls had effected the first American penetration of the Soviet compound. I wondered about Yuri's reaction when he found my embassy calling card inside the box of cookies.

I found out when Yuri confronted me during a reception at the Swedish embassy. To the amusement of nearby diplomats, Yuri lambasted me for "using children to do CIA dirty work." It was obvious I was wasting my time on the thick-skinned Yuri, who was too hard core.

My last run at Yuri was during the International Trade Fair, which took place every December. Various countries promoted and exhibited their national products and specialties, the Swedes flogging glassware, the Japanese cameras, the Chinese their silk, and the Russians tractors and vodka. The Americans, because of "budget limitations," had to be satisfied with a plywood mock-up of the New York City skyline plus four Georgia O'Keefe reproductions. The fair was a mecca of espionage activities and targets of opportunity. The KGB chief sent out his case officers disguised as "fair guides," Mossad agents from Israel posing as "buyers" plied Arab nations' pavilions, and Chinese Communists went about pilfering brochures from the Taiwan exhibit.

On opening day, I went directly to the Soviet pavilion, walking along the red carpet lined with hammer and sickle flags. Yuri was standing behind a long table with bottles of different-colored vodkas arranged in ten-pin triangles. He didn't look particularly pleased to see me approaching, but because he couldn't turn me away, he grudgingly offered me a glass of vodka.

I offered a toast to "Mother Russia," *za vache zdorobie*, thanked Yuri, and emptied the glass. I turned to walk away, but Yuri had decided he wasn't going to let his American counterpart off that easily. He told me to try the "top-quality" yellow vodka. I drank and gave another toast to the Motherland. Yuri then urged me to sample the red vodka, which he said went down best when chased with 150-proof Stolichnaya.

Yuri was trying to get me drunk, and I knew if I didn't break away from my KGB counterpart with his rainbow of vodkas, he would succeed. I grabbed Yuri by the arm and insisted he come over to visit the American pavilion. He tried to beg off, but I persisted, urging him in a loud voice to permit me to repay the hospitality of our grand Russian ally.

I then guided him to our pavilion to a table in the back, where I had stashed a bottle of Jack Daniels for "special guests." I poured out a double shot for Yuri, who tossed it down, and before he could protest, I poured him a second double shot. When I offered him a third drink, he shattered his glass by slamming it down on the table. He then abruptly turned around and left, without even bothering to offer a toast to Uncle Sam.

I was still woozy from Yuri's vodka and went out to the car, where Nick, my driver, was waiting. I climbed in and told Nick to drive me home, then promptly fell asleep. I had barely dropped off when the car stopped. Nick had turned around and told me to look out the window. A Mercedes with CD-37 plates had gone off the road and was sitting in the middle of a field. A figure was leaning against the Mercedes, emptying his bladder on the rear wheel. It was Yuri.

I got out of my car and walked across the field and came up behind Yuri. When I tapped him on the shoulder. The Russian jerked around in surprise and immediately tried zipping up his fly. His privates became caught in his zipper, and

Yuri cried out, and then, when he recognized who had tapped on his shoulder, he yelled even louder, frantically tugging at his zipper.

Yuri was finally able to zip up his pants, but he was still weaving unsteadily. I put my hand on his shoulder, trying to steady him, and offered him a ride. He shucked my hand off, growling that he didn't need my help because he had his own car. Just then the radiator of the Mercedes let out a hissing noise and the front wheels sank into the wet ground.

Finally, realizing his car wasn't going anywhere, Yuri grudgingly let me guide him across the field and up the bank to my car. Nick was standing, holding the back door open, and he helped me get the protesting Yuri inside. I quietly told Nick to drive us to my house. When we arrived at my house, Yuri was still grumbling. I helped him out of the car, led him inside, and sat him in a chair facing the Christmas tree we had just decorated the night before. I then went out to the kitchen, brought out two glasses of eggnog, and handed one to Yuri, which he immediately drank.

When he put his glass down, I told him it was customary during the Yuletide season for guests to hang an ornament on the Christmas tree. I held out a shiny red ball, helped him out of the chair, and guided him over to the tree. Yuri mumbled something about heathen customs, but finally hung the ornament on a branch of the tree, unaware that Joy had just taken a picture with my Polaroid.

Yuri again insisted on leaving, but I stalled him long enough so that I could find a copy of the *Reader's Digest*, which featured an article on "The KGB in America." I slipped the magazine into the pocket of his overcoat, helped him out to the car, and told Nick to drive Yuri to the Soviet embassy.

A half hour later, Nick returned and told me what had happened when Yuri arrived at his embassy. The security guard, obviously surprised to see a KGB officer arriving in an American embassy car, rushed down the steps to open the car door. Yuri almost fell out of the car before the guard caught him, the *Readers Digest* and the Polaroid photo dropping out of his pocket. The security guard quickly picked up the magazine and photo and then helped the KGB deputy up the steps into the embassy.

Leaving Yuri at the entrance to his embassy in a U.S. embassy car was like leaving a wreath for an intended Mafia victim. Three weeks later Yuri was sent back to Moscow, a blot on his KGB escutcheon.

Although chances were I would never know, it was possible that one day Yuri might conclude that a defector's life might have more to offer than being a disgraced officer in his own service.

Do svedana, Yuri, good-bye.

The Defector

Defectors. All of us. While we are fresh, we are handed round and used.
When our tricks are known and we are past our prime, we are tossed
onto the rubbish heap.

—JOHN LE CARRE, *Absolute Friends*

One target literally fell into the Station's hands. A drunk Soviet crashed his car
through the gates of the American embassy. The Marine guard, who pulled him
out of the car, heard him mumble something about "asylum."

Most defectors resist being "turned around" and sent back to work in place.
They resist because they wouldn't have defected in the first place if they knew they
would have to go back. In the case of the gate crasher, he had a good reason for
not going back. He had absconded with his embassy's petty cash fund and blown
it all at the local casino.

We weren't going to turn him away, but we had to do something with him
right away. We spirited "Dimitri" out of the embassy and stashed him in a spare
bedroom in my house. Meanwhile, the Soviet ambassador launched a protest with
the Samudran Foreign Ministry about "foreign agents" kidnapping one of their
diplomats. The Foreign Ministry "took note" of the Soviet ambassador's protest
and passed it along to the Security Service.

While we waited for a decision to be made about the defector, I stayed at
home and took meals into his bedroom. Karl, a Russian-speaking case officer,
came over to talk to Dimitri and make him feel more at ease. While all this activity was going on in the house, including visits from the station chief, I overheard
a conversation between Gray and Megan talking about the "funny goings-on."
"Megan, you know why Bill and Karl keep coming by the house? Because that
missing Russian that everyone is talking about is hiding out in our house!"

When it was decided that the defector should be sent to the United States,
Karl and I accompanied him. After we landed and were saying good-bye, Dimitri,
who had become attached to us, looked so worried that the officers who had met
us suggested we take him out to dinner and they would pick him up later. We
drove to a restaurant in nearby Falls Church that had a band and floorshow that
might help to ease Dimitri's transition. We had just been seated and ordered a
round of drinks when all the lights went out. The worst cloudburst in fifty years
dumped a foot of rain and flooded streets, knocking out power in Washington
and Virginia. We sat in the dark for almost an hour before they were able to bring
out candles. I noticed the wide-eyed expression on Dimitri's face. The Russian
was probably wondering if he had made the right choice in defecting to a "land of
plenty" that had no electric power.

Dimitri was eventually given a new identity and resettled in the American Midwest. He brooded about his wife and son back in Moscow and started to drink heavily, calling his case officer to come to his rescue. This went on for almost a year until he made contact for the last time. He was phoning from the Soviet consulate in New York and said he had decided to turn himself in. He was calling to say good-bye.

The last I heard of Dimitri was a year later, when another defector reported that Dimitri had resurfaced in Moscow and was giving lectures at the KGB Academy on "CIA Brainwashing Techniques."

Maria

Since Yuri had undoubtedly "burned" me with the Soviet embassy, I would have to recruit an access agent to get at my next Soviet target.

Maria was dark haired, tall, and, with her smooth, olive complexion, stunning. Her Russian father had immigrated to China in the 1920s as part of the White Russian diaspora. From her father, Maria inherited her height, sharp tongue, and volatile temper; from her Chinese mother, high cheekbones and a slight epicanthic slant to her eyes.

I first heard and then saw Maria playing tennis. She was leaping like a gazelle around the court, chasing lobs, smashing returns, and cursing in a mix of Russian, Samudran, and English. Her partner was a Soviet embassy diplomat, which surprised me, because Soviet officials normally shunned White Russians, whom they considered "closet czarists." Maria must have been an exception, because she was often seen at Soviet embassy functions.

The next time I saw Maria she was sitting beside the Hotel Samudra swimming pool, conversing with a Russian, who I recognized from a rogues' gallery photo as a GRU colonel, Boris Ossofsky, head of the Soviet Military Mission in Samudra.

Boris

In contrast to most of the burly Soviets in Jakarta, Boris Ossofsky was delicate, fine-featured, and frail looking. His blotched complexion indicated he was sensitive to the tropical sun, which he tried to keep at bay with dark glasses and a wide-brim straw hat. Boris had a gentle face and, according to what Maria told me later, spoke soft classical Russian unlike the guttural patois spoken by the new apparatchik generation.

When I observed her at the pool laughing and whispering with Boris, it was obvious Maria had excellent rapport with a potential new target. I hadn't considered the possibility of a White Russian as an access agent. Maria, however, was apparently well liked by the Soviets, who often invited her to receptions at their embassy and vied for her as a doubles partner.

Maria would make an ideal access agent, although she would bristle at the term and prefer "soul mate" or "friendly intermediary." Maria and Boris. My adrenalin was pumping.

—⁂—

At the tennis courts, I noticed that between sets Maria had gone over to talk to an American who happened to be a friend of mine at the embassy. She played tennis with Maria and agreed to introduce me. Maria gripped my hand hard as if she was grasping a tennis racket. Her English was excellent but rapid fire, and I had a hard time breaking in. At one point in the conversation, she said she heard Americans were great dog lovers, and she was looking for a dog as a pet for her children.

I told Maria a friend of mine had recently had a litter of Labrador puppies shipped in from Australia. I would ask him to give me one for Maria. The friend in question was the local Pan American Airlines representative, who was a good source of gossip on the comings and goings of foreign visitors. I was sure he would spring a puppy for me if I asked him.

A few weeks later I presented Maria with a Labrador puppy, which paved the way for a lasting friendship. Maria liked to gossip and was a fount of information on the international community, especially the extramarital affairs of members of the diplomatic community, including several prominent ambassadors.

Maria was not as forthcoming with me about her Soviet friends. She usually cut me off when I brought up the subject of the Russians, telling me Americans don't know the difference between Russians and Soviets. She asked how "you Americans, with your Elvis Presley, Coca-Cola, and Hollywood could possibly be interested in the land of Tchaikovsky, Dostoevsky, and the Bolshoi."

When I brought up the Cold War, she said it was nothing more than a "stupid squabble between overgrown bullies bragging about who had the most nukes."

Later on I decided I would try a different approach. I told Maria I had a friend in the United States who was working toward a doctorate in Russian studies. His doctoral thesis focused on profiles of Soviet citizens. He had completed profiles on Russian émigré defectors, exiled writers, and dissidents living in the United States. But they were anomalies. He wanted profiles of Soviets such as those living abroad and asked me if I could help him in his research. I was about to go on, but Maria, seeing through my charade, interrupted. "You say you have a friend in America who wants to know about the kinds of Russians living in Samudra for some paper he's writing? You can do better than that!"

My drooping fig leaf left me vulnerable, and I braced for another tirade on my "lack of sensitivity" about the Russian soul. It didn't come. Instead, Maria asked if I had a particular Russian in mind whose id I wanted her to dissect. "Like Boris, maybe?"

Maria probably didn't believe there was a professor, but it didn't matter. She told me, "OK. I'll do your Freud thing and look into the soul of my friend, Boris. I always wanted to be a couch doctor!"

Couch Doctor

The character profile was a recent Headquarters requirement. New times required new methods. Psychologists had extended their Rorshach tentacles into field operations, and a psychological profile was required on any prospective Soviet recruitment candidate. Twenty pages of questions from breast-feeding and thumb sucking, to fingernail chewing and masturbation. There were two pages of questions about dreams.

Maria liked the idea of probing Boris id, telling me, "You want to know what Boris thinks about his mommy's boobies? I'll get him talking about 'Mother Russia' and go from there. Masturbation? I'll ask him how he copes in Samudra with his wife back in Moscow!"

I passed Maria the questions piecemeal to avoid overloading her and making Boris suspicious. She was intrigued by the questions, but I cautioned her that probing too deeply might set off alarm bells, leading Boris to clam up or even become hostile. Maria told me to relax. Her Slavic instincts would tell her how to play Boris without making him suspicious. I should have given Maria more credit. She was almost professional in eliciting answers from Boris to even the most sensitive questions. Boris liked talking to Maria about himself, and in a matter of weeks I had enough material for the psychologists to chew on.

The feedback from Headquarters was excellent, highlighting a number of Boris's vulnerabilities I had overlooked, particularly his chronic hypochondria. Foreigners stationed in the tropics, with lots of time on their hands, have a tendency to develop symptoms of a variety of tropical diseases. In his conversations with Maria, Boris had alluded to a variety of ailments he had experienced, including boils, rashes, stomach pains, and mysterious blotches on his skin. He had obsessions about coming down with a fatal disease such as dengue fever or cerebral malaria. He had dreams about succumbing to the dreaded yellow monkey disease.

Boris needed an American doctor.

Doctor Andy

The time had come to cut Maria out of the operation. I thanked for her help with Boris and told her that she could now stop playing couch doctor and go back to just being friends with Boris.

Doctor Andrew, "Andy," was the American embassy physician. He had helped me once with Mikolai, a Yugoslav friend who had come to my house late one night covered with blood. Mikolai was sobbing uncontrollably and it was several minutes before he calmed down enough to tell me he had just killed his wife, Jill.

I was worried about Mikolai's bleeding and called Andy, who immediately came over. He examined Mikolai and told me that, despite being soaked with blood, my Yugoslav friend was unhurt. We concluded the blood must have come from his wife, and the three of us rushed over to Mikolai's house. Jill lay sprawled on the patio in a pool of blood. The tiles were littered with broken glass, several shards protruding from her hair. Andy knelt down and felt her pulse. Jill was in shock but still alive, and like in one of those old westerns, Andy told Mikolai to quickly bring towels and a basin of warm water.

After Andy cleaned and bandaged her wounds, Jill began to come around. Andy told Mikolai his wife had suffered a concussion from the bottle of Campari he had smashed over her head. The Campari also accounted for most of the "blood" splattered over the patio. Mikolai sheepishly admitted his Slavic temper had gotten the better of him. Andy gave Mikolai a sedative to give his wife and told him to bring her by the embassy the next day so he could check on her condition. Andy and I then went back to my house.

I apologized to Andy for rousting him out in the middle of the night, but Andy insisted it was a welcome change from his daily routine of treating bored wives with imaginary ailments, diaper-rashed infants, and worried husbands checking for signs of gonorrhea. He said if I had any more interesting cases to give him a call.

I took Andy up on his offer sooner than expected. Going through Boris's file, two items caught my attention: his hypochondria and the address of his apartment. Boris lived at #10 Jalan Baru, the same street Dr. Andy lived on.

I asked Andy over for dinner to thank him for helping me out with my Yugoslav friend. After dinner, I asked Andy if he could help me out again, this time with a Russian military officer. I asked him if his Hippocratic oath of confidentiality would apply in this case, which was highly sensitive. He said that secrecy was as much a part of his profession as it was of mine.

I told Andy about Boris and about his hypochondria, which would make him amenable to an approach from an American doctor. I briefed him on what we knew about Boris, his habits, and the location of his apartment. I wanted Andy to contact the Soviet, develop a friendship with him, and later introduce me.

The plan for contacting Boris was simple. We knew that Boris went for a walk every evening after he came back from work. He walked along a path by the river, stopping frequently to look at the fishing boats or the Samudran sunset. Andy should begin walking along the same path Boris took and inevitably they would meet. Andy should not acknowledge Boris the first time their paths crossed, but later he should nod to him and wish him a good evening. Later he could try to start a conversation with Boris, and eventually he could sit beside him on one of the benches on the promontory where Boris usually stopped to watch the sunset.

I gave Andy a photograph of Boris and asked him to keep me posted.

Two weeks later Andy came by my house, and I could tell he was very pleased with himself. He told me that he and Boris had already become friends. He had passed Boris several times along the path until one afternoon Boris asked Andy to sit with him on the promontory.

They didn't talk much at first, concentrating on watching the praus. Boris commented that they were probably similar to those described by Marco Polo in his thirteenth-century journals. He seemed to be well read, and they conversed on a variety of subjects except for world affairs.

The sunset watch became almost a ritual, until one afternoon Boris didn't arrive on the promontory. He showed up the next day later than usual complaining of stomach cramps, which he said had kept him from coming the day before. The cramps still gnawed at him, so Andy confided that he was a doctor and would bring some medicine for Boris the following afternoon, which he did. The next day Boris told Andy his cramps had disappeared, and he was so pleased he invited Andy to come to his apartment over the weekend, saying they could watch the sun go down from his terrace while drinking his own elixir of vodka and caviar.

"How's that for Operation Hippocrates? We sit there watching the sun go down over the Jaya River and he tells me all about the sunsets over the Volga! Then he wonders if I can balance his metabolism and expunge the nasty larvae corroding his intestines. Next thing I'll become his confessor. Now, about my fee—"

I encouraged Andy to continue the relationship. The two men soon became close, alternating "consultations" and chess at Andy's house with vodka sunset watches at Boris's apartment. Boris began telling Andy intimate details of his life, details he hadn't even told Maria. When he looked over the trees at the minarets of the mosques in the distance, he told Andy how much he missed Moscow with its Orthodox cupolas and the ice-crusted Volga. For his part, Andy treated Boris's ulcer, soothed his rheumatoid pains, and elevated his metabolism to its maximum.

It was time for Andy to introduce his "friend" to Boris. Andy wasn't enthusiastic and made excuses about delaying the introduction. I reminded Andy of our original agreement and assured him the introduction wouldn't affect his friendship with Boris or tarnish his physician's credentials. We would play it out as a "good-cop-bad-cop" routine—Andy the good friend/physician and me the "bad" bureaucrat/political officer. All I would ask of Andy, once the introduction had taken place, was to keep me advised of any feedback about "the American political officer he had met at Andy's house."

Andy was relieved he could be able to continue his relationship with Boris without being tainted. He was certain Boris would tell him what he thought of me, and if he suspected my motives.

We arranged for me to be at Andy's house one night when Boris was due to come over for a game of chess. He introduced me as an embassy officer who had come by to pick up some pills. I let a couple of weeks go by, and for my second meeting, I told Andy I wanted to talk to Boris alone. When the Russian came by, I would tell him that Andy was out on a call, that he would be back shortly, and that I was just minding his office until he came back.

When Boris arrived, he seemed undecided about whether to wait for Andy or leave. I offered him a drink from Andy's bar, assuring him the doctor would be back shortly. Boris accepted the offer of a drink and agreed to wait until Andy returned. Boris pointed to the chessboard and asked if I played. I told him the game was too complicated for me, but my son, Gray, played and often talked about the great Russian chess players. I added that I was sure he would be very excited if he could play with a Russian chess master like Boris.

It wasn't a subtle ploy, but I wasn't sure I'd get another crack at Boris. The chess gambit would give me an opportunity to talk to Boris without Andy being around. Boris smiled and didn't reply.

When Andy returned, and I told him I had asked Boris to play chess with my son, Andy picked up on the cue and told Boris he ought to take me up on the invitation and inspire a future American chess champion. Andy added that he would be happy to help arrange the match. I suggested a time and date, and although I could see Boris didn't like being pressured, he agreed and told Andy to arrange it.

The day of the proposed match, I wasn't sure Boris would show. Andy told me it was all arranged and that he had given Boris my address, but that he knew the Russian wasn't enthusiastic about coming to my house. Boris surprised me, arriving at the time agreed on. I introduced him to Gray, and the two sat down to play. I went to my study until the match was over and Boris got ready to leave. I offered him a drink, but he declined. He said he had enjoyed playing with Gray and they had arranged a rematch.

Boris came to the house several times afterward to play chess with Gray, but on only one occasion did he agree to stay for a drink. I tried talking to him about Russia, the competition in space, and nuclear proliferation, but Boris said he wasn't interested in world politics.

When at one point he expressed an interest in the outdoors, I gave him some copies of the *National Geographic*, featuring the wilderness attractions of Glacier and Yellowstone Parks. I told Boris it was unfortunate the Cold War prevented us from traveling to our respective countries. Boris changed the subject and left, taking the copies of *National Geographic* with him.

After one of their chess matches, Gray had to leave quickly for a scout meeting. I told Boris this time he didn't have any excuse for not staying, and I handed him a drink and asked him to sit down. We talked about the rigors of living in the tropics and being away from our homes for extended periods of time. I again brought up the subject of relations between the United States and the USSR, and before he could change the subject, I said that "as an air force officer," Boris was aware of the consequences of a nuclear war, which could be set off by miscalculations or misunderstandings. I thought that mention of his air force affiliation would get a rise out of Boris, who had always passed himself off to me as a minor embassy official, but it didn't. He said that even if I were right, he didn't like discussing world politics, which didn't interest him.

When Boris came for his final match with Gray, I again asked him to stay briefly so we could talk. I promised not to keep him, but there was a "confidential matter" I wanted to discuss with him. Boris agreed to stay briefly because it was the last time he would be seeing me. Adjourning to my study, I asked Boris if he had ever thought about coming to the United States. I said that since he had been kind enough to teach my son the finer points of chess, I wondered if there was something I could do for him. I said I was just "thinking out loud" but wondered if in the future Boris might take a leave of absence and spend a year or more in the United States. I was sure he could obtain a high-paid consultancy with an American aerospace firm such as Boeing or United Technologies. He could have a farm on the steppes of Nebraska, a vacation dacha in the Rockies.

Boris began to look uneasy, so before he could break off our conversation and leave, I reminded him I was just "thinking out loud." I was surprised that, for once, Boris didn't seem angry. I could see, however, that he was uncomfortable with the conversation.

He finished his drink and said good-bye. I asked if we could meet again to continue our discussion. He shook hands but didn't reply.

The operation was down to the wire. I drafted a message to Headquarters asking for authorization to recruit "RUVOLGA." The pitch would emphasize the dangers of a nuclear confrontation being triggered by false or misinformation. RUVOLGA, as a senior air force officer, was knowledgeable of Soviet nuclear plans and activities. If he could keep us advised of those plans and intentions, he would be well rewarded.

The message advised that RUVOLGA would not be pressured at this meeting. He would be given time to reflect on the proposal and another meeting would be arranged to "continue the discussion." The message said, "If RUVOLGA agrees to another meeting, will offer him substantial cash sum to be put in escrow in a Swiss bank account. He would also be guaranteed eventual resettlement in the U.S. with his family."

Although headquarters authorized making a recruitment pitch to RUVOLGA, the pitch didn't work out as planned. A cable was sent to Headquarters summarizing the abortive operation.

RUVOLGA listened to the initial pitch, shaking his head and angrily scolding St. Martin for abusing their friendship. St. Martin, hoping that RUVOLGA was merely exercising his "right of first refusal," nodded and said he understood. After calming RUVOLGA down, he asked him if they could meet one more time. RUVOLGA seemed to be mollified and agreed to a "final" meeting, saying he would call St. Martin.

When RUVOLGA called, he advised St. Martin that he was the embassy duty officer and had to remain at home by his phone. He suggested St. Martin come by his apartment and they could discuss "the matter in question" further.

Checkmate

I'd lived a long enough life to learn my lessons on the awful and frightful ways this world can be, [but] I had at least one more lesson ahead.
— J. BROWN, *Decorations in a Ruined Cemetery*

The cable went on to describe St. Martin's recollection of the subsequent turn of events.

Although I was disturbed by the proposed change of venue, I told the chief I believed I had to go through with the meeting to find out what RUVOLGA's final decision was. The operation was down to the wire, and I wanted to find out if RUVOLGA had accepted the pitch and if not to terminate the operation.

When I arrived at RUVOLGA's apartment, a Soviet whom I had never seen before opened the door and led me inside. RUVOLGA was nowhere to be seen. Sitting behind a table in the middle of the room, another Soviet was thumbing through a dossier. He looked up and said, "Yours is an interesting file, St. Martin. Even though you have a history of running provocative operations against Soviet citizens, I commend your aggressive style, including your attempt to recruit RUVOLGA.

"Now I have a proposition for you. You will ostensibly be allowed to recruit RUVOLGA and we will even permit him to sign a contract to that effect. In exchange, you will agree to cooperate with us and provide information on American intelligence activities in Southeast Asia.

"In return for your 'cooperation,' I am offering you twenty-five thousand U.S. dollars," he said, shoving a brown envelope across the table.

"If you do not accept this generous offer, the Soviet ambassador will lodge a formal protest with the Samudran Foreign Office about your attempt to recruit a Soviet official on Samudran soil. The Samudran press will also be advised of your attempt to subvert a Soviet officer."

St. Martin reached over and took the envelope, saying he needed time to think over the offer. The Soviet replied that St. Martin had twenty-four hours in which to decide.

Headquarters was advised that in light of this unexpected turn of events, and to avoid any adverse fallout from the RUVOLGA operation, St. Martin would leave Samudra as soon as possible to visit "critically ill" mother in the U.S.

The twenty-five thousand dollars, probably counterfeit, was pouched to Headquarters.

Soviet operations were put on hold, and the file on RUVOLGA was closed.

PART III
The Last Covert Action

CHAPTER 10: **Buwana**

Once every few years, even now, I catch the scent of Africa. It makes
me want to keen, sing, clap up thunder, lie down at the foot of a tree
and let the worms take whatever of me they can still use.

—BARBARA KINGSOLVER, *The Poisonwood Bible*

Buwana was discovered a decade before Columbus sailed for America by a
Portuguese explorer seeking Prester John's "Lost Kingdom." Sitting astride
the equator, Buwana is almost the size of Western Europe. Its central plateau
is equatorial forest, and in the east mountains rise up to sixteen thousand feet.

There are several hundred tribes in Buwana, including early pygmy inhabitants. Its jungles and rain forests shelter a variety of wild animals, including gorillas,
rhinos, and leopards. The country has a plentiful supply of diamonds, copper, and
most of the world's cobalt, making it one of the richest countries in the world.

The Congo River, second in length only to the Amazon, flows for three thousand miles through Buwana, cascading down over a series of waterfalls to Stanley
Pool, where globs of water hyacinth temporarily impede its flow, then picks up
speed again and crashes over Livingston Falls and a series of rapids until it finally
empties into the Atlantic.

The river was immortalized by Henry Stanley, a *New York Herald* journal-
ist, whose search for a famous missionary ended with the celebrated line "Dr.
Livingston, I presume?" His African explorations also caught the attention of King
Leopold II of Belgium, who later "annexed" the country as his private fiefdom.

The Final Call

Chief of Station, Buwana. I had looked forward to running an African outpost,
conjuring up muscled Paul Robesons chanting as they poled their pirogues past
sunning crocodiles and splashing hippos.

The pace would be slow and easy. No more guerrilla tail chasing, insurgen-
cies, and counterinsurgencies, winning hearts and minds. Back to the basics of
chasing spies, collecting intelligence, and, in the case of Buwana, keeping the
president happy.

Of the children, only Megan accompanied us to Buwana. Laurie was studying for a degree in human resources, Kent was at the University of New Hampshire, and Gray was taking a year off from the University of Montana, putting college "on hold" while he thumbed his way through Central and South America. After a year south of the border in Central America, Gray arrived in Buwana and got a job working on the Inga Dam power project. He and a friend later embarked on an African journey, traveling by boat up the Congo River, walking and bumming rides through the Central African Republic and Chad, then on up to Algeria and Morocco, where their safari ended and Gray came down with hepatitis.

Megan went off to school in Switzerland at Le Mans in Geneva, returning to Buwana between semesters. During a summer break, her two best friends, a brother and sister from Holland, were hit and killed by a drunken truck driver.

Megan later returned to Le Mans, where she graduated, with her parents in attendance.

For the new chief of station, the pace for the first six months was as expected, slow and easy. There was a brief flurry of activity with the "rumble in the jungle," the world championship boxing match between Cassius Clay and George Foreman. Journalists and fight aficionados descended on the capital to watch Foreman train and Ali "sting-like-a-bee." The bout was delayed for three weeks because of squabbling over contracts, but the two fighters eventually squared off at three in the morning to accommodate U.S. television viewers.

Ali retained the diamond-studded world champion's belt, and then the two fighters, retinues, and fans left before the rains came and Buwana returned to normal.

Then the "OPERATIONAL IMMEDIATE" landed on my desk.

The Dark Continent

We carry within us the wonders we seek without us:
There is all Africa, and her prodigies in us.

—SIR THOMAS BROWN

Over the years, policy makers had largely ignored Africa. In the 1960s there had been a flare-up in the Belgian Congo when the rebels forced our officer in Kisangani to eat the American flag, but the Agency then became preoccupied with Southeast Asia and lost interest in Africa.

After the fall of Saigon and the cessation of its operations in Southeast Asia, the Agency decided to pull in its paramilitary horns and go back to concentrating on its bread and butter tasks of gathering intelligence. The paramilitary poltergeists would soon be resurrected however. Operational storm clouds were building over Africa.

CHAPTER 11: **Angafula**

The last vestige of colonialism in Africa, Angafula was a Texas-size colony that lay two hundred miles south of the equator. Independence fevers had bypassed the Portuguese colony until the early 1970s, when long-silenced tribal drums began thumping war calls for freedom.

The reverberations were picked up and relayed along the Potomac into the office of the "Metternich" of American foreign policy, who was deeply emerged in thought. Dr. Heinzleman asked about the source of these reverberations, and when told it was a Portuguese colony in Africa, he asked for an immediate briefing, which went as follows:

Angafula boasts a four-hundred mile coastline of white sandy beaches. Its tropical forests are interspersed with coffee plantations. Elsewhere in the country are mineral deposits of copper, uranium, and diamonds. Angafula boasts a good infrastructure of primary and secondary roads, ports, rail lines, and airfields.

The Angafulans are friendly and easygoing but prone to frequent bouts of internecine tribal warfare.

Demonstrations against the colonial Salazar government in Portugal have recently broken out in Lunda, the capital city. Three major groups are in the forefront of these demonstrations:

The Front for the Liberation of Angafula (FLA), led by "Reverend" Rebello, a mystic missionary

The Union for the Total Independence of Angafula (UTIA), led by Juan Sanchez, a former soccer star.

The Popular Movement to Free Angafula (PMFA), led by Augustus Sappho, a physician, poet, and alumnus of the Patrice Lumumba

University in Moscow. Sappho's organization receives substantial financial and material support from the Soviet Union.

(Comment: The Soviets, whose geopolitical ambitions in Africa are well known, have targeted Angafula to gain an initial foothold on the continent. In return for their support to the PMFA, they are allowed to operate openly in Angafula without interference from the lame duck Portuguese government, which still administers the colony. The Portuguese colonial administrators, resigned to the colony's independence, support Sappho and the PMFA.

(The Soviets assume the United States is too traumatized from the Vietnam War to interfere in Africa and feel free to pursue their expansionist goals in Angafula without American interference.)

The allusion to a "traumatized United States" rankled National Security Adviser Heinzleman, who knew more about Soviet geopolitical ambitions than anyone in Washington. He drafted a memorandum for the president, urging action "when our determination is being questioned, to counter Soviet moves in Angafula and preempt its loss to Communism of this key African country."

The Last Covert Action was about to begin.

The Last Covert Action

A perfect tragedy is the noblest production of human nature.
—JOSEPH ADDISON, The Spectator

I received the cable at midnight, ordering me to be prepared to implement a large covert action program to support two independence movements across the river in neighboring Angafula.

I was to brief President Bongo on the program and ask for his support in providing cover and logistical support. The cable said further details would follow.

I could hardly believe it. The "funeral-baked meats" were still warm on the table and we were off again. Another clarion call to covert action by the producers of the Bay of Pigs and the saga of the montagnards. Saddle up for a last crusade. Hopefully, the Angafulans weren't aware of our last crusade, which lay in tatters on the Plaines des Jarres and in the highlands of Indochina.

Familiar phrases threaded through the "details" that followed: "sheep-dipped advisers," "nonattributable" weapons, "sterile" air support.

Since the operation was to be staged out of Buwana, my first task was to brief President Bongo and then ask him to provide cover and logistical support.

Bongo

Bongo Wa Za Zenga, the "all powerful warrior," was christened John Wishful when he was born in 1930. Bongo was educated in mission schools, where he learned to speak French and, according to his teachers, was difficult to control, respecting only the authority of Mama Selo, his mother. Troublesome boys like Bongo were sent off to the Force Publique, King Leopold's private army. Bongo served for seven years in the Force Publique, where he read voraciously and studied military tactics and history.

When his service contract was over, he married the fourteen-year-old Anne Marie Lisette and in 1955 went to Brussels, where he dabbled in journalism. In Brussels he came in contact with Buwanan intellectuals, including Patrice Bulanda with whom he became friends and later assassinated.

In 1965 Colonel Bongo ousted President Suwango, declared himself president, and then ruled the country for the next thirty-two years.

President and Marshal of the Army Bongo was ambitious, ruthless, generous, street-smart, and endowed with a prodigious memory. I remember meetings with Bongo when I would be talking to him while he listened to "Europe 1" on the radio and talked on the phone with his generals. After ten minutes or more, he would hang up and resume our conversation, referring back to my last phrase before he had broken off the conversation.

Le Guide, as he liked to be called, fostered the legend that when he was a young boy, he had killed a leopard. After he became president, he wore a leopard-skin toque cocked on the side of his head and was seldom without his carved ivory walking stick, which he used both as a pointer and to jab into dozing subordinates. He insisted that all government ministers and officials wear the abacos ("down with the suit"), a jacket with no lapels, symbolizing Buwana's break from colonial rule.

Our "special relationship" with Bongo dated back to the 1960s, when he credited our chief of station with saving him during an assassination attempt. The special relationship continued with COSs that followed and was not always appreciated by the American ambassador. The ambassador is the designated contact for a chief of state, although the protocol was often skirted in Buwana. Early on in my tour in Buwana, the ambassador made it clear I was to keep him advised before and after any meeting with the president, which I did. Unfortunately, President Bongo and his minister didn't like the ambassador's recommendations that the government cut down the profligate spending habits of its ministers. Bongo staged a phony coup, Le Coup Manque, which he used as an excuse to have the ambassador recalled. The same ambassador went on to a distinguished career as ambassador to a number of capitals, where his talents were more appreciated.

—ɱ—

I had developed a fairly good relationship with Bongo, who frequently summoned me for early-morning meetings at his hilltop residence located next to the barracks of the Presidential Guard. It was also just up the hill from his private zoo, where giant crocodiles basked in the sun and warned off unwelcome visitors.

The president's residence overlooked Stanley Pool and the capital of the Republic of Congo on opposite riverbank. My meetings with the president were informal, and I usually was called when Bongo wanted to relay his views to Washington or to lecture me about our foreign policy missteps in Africa.

Bongo could also be ruthless. During one of our meetings, he scolded me for my "close association" with one of his officers. He said he suspected the officer of being "disloyal," and I assured Bongo I had never discussed politics with the officer, who was helping us out on logistics problems having to do with our joint program. Bongo, however, being himself an inveterate coup plotter, was convinced the captain was plotting against him and had him executed.

Bongo could also be disarmingly warm and friendly and often invited me to dinner with his family. During one such dinner, I was seated near the end of a long table along with a dozen or more members of Bongo's extended family. A chicken bone became lodged in my throat, and I couldn't breathe. All my efforts to dislodge the bone with heaping mouthfuls of rice and glasses of beer were unsuccessful. I began to choke, and with my eyes watering, it suddenly occurred to me that this is how it would end, expiring at Le Guide's table with a chicken bone lodged in my throat.

Fortunately, Bongo's wife, Anne Marie, who was sitting at the other end of the table, noticed my predicament. She got up and came over, and standing behind my chair, banged on my back between the shoulder blades. She hit me hard several times until the bone popped out of my mouth and dropped onto the plate. Anne Marie then returned to her seat beside the president, who was still recounting an anecdote about the tribal warfare in Belgium between the Flemish and Walloons and hadn't noticed the near expiration of the station chief.

—ɱ—

The day after the cable arrived about the proposed program, I telephoned Bongo's aide to arrange a meeting. The president's sixth sense probably alerted him that something important was in the wind, because his aide immediately called back to say that he would see me right away.

I began by passing greetings from the American president, who Bongo had met during one of his visits to Washington. I also passed him regards from the other senior officials, whom Bongo had also met on his visits to Washington. I then briefed Bongo on Washington's concerns about recent Soviet moves in Africa and particularly Angafula and the alarming prospect of a Soviet puppet state across the border from Buwana.

The president nodded and asked me to continue. I told him I had come to discuss a program to thwart Soviet ambitions in Angafula. The program, which would provide support for the FLA and UTIA independence groups, would, if the president agreed, have its logistics base in Buwana. I asked President Bongo if he would provide cover for the operation as part of his regular military assistance program and logistical support to include quartermaster personnel, warehouses, and special access to the Bintang airport and Katapi harbor.

Bongo replied that he would be glad "to help his friends in Washington" and provide whatever assistance was needed. I told him he would incidentally be receiving additional M-16 rifles and other items to augment his military assistance program. Potentates are usually pleased when their status and power are recognized, and Bongo was no exception. He smiled, tapping his ivory cane on the floor and reiterating his assurances about being happy to help his friends in Washington. As I was leaving, he asked when he could expect the additional M-16s.

Rebello and Sanchez

Having gotten Bongo's approval to support the program, I went to discuss it with the two Angafulan leaders.

Rebello, the FLA leader, was born in 1923 in the Angafulan province of Sao Salvador, across the Buwanan border. Raised by missionaries, he attended Baptist mission schools until 1940. He joined several independence groups and became president of the largest one, the Front for the Liberation of Angafula. The movement was supported from its base in Buwana across the river from Rebello's Angafula. The movement's first foreign minister was Juan Sanchez, who later broke from the FLA to form his own group.

Rebello was dour, ascetic, and uncompromising. Although he was a staunch anticommunist, he hadn't hesitated to turn to Red China for aid in arming and training two companies of his FLA partisans. His rationale for accepting aid from Communist China was "the enemy of my enemy is my friend," and Red China, at the time, was the enemy of the Soviet Union.

Juan Sanchez founded UTIA shortly after he left Rebello's FLA. Born in 1934, Sanchez was an Ovimbundu, the largest tribal group in Angafula. Like Rebello,

Sanchez was the product of missionary schools. In his early twenties he went to Europe to study political science and medicine before returning to Angafula to organize the UTIA.

Sanchez was as charismatic as Rebello was dour. He had been a champion soccer player and was a spellbinding speaker. His beard, green fatigues, and oratorical skills invited comparison to Fidel Castro, the Cuban leader who would one day send troops to fight him.

While Rebello drew his support from the region bordering Buwana, Sanchez' tribal base was in the interior of Angafula, where most of the rubber and coffee plantations as well as diamond mines were located. It was also in the region through which the important Benguela railroad ran linking Angafula with the rest of Africa.

Sanchez mistrusted Rebello because of the FLA leader's close ties to President Bongo, but he saved his real contempt for Sappho, the "Red Poet," whose verses Sanchez called nothing more than "toilet-stall graffiti."

I had no trouble selling our program to the two leaders. Both were pleased to learn the United States was going to provide support to their respective movements, but they were less than pleased when they learned President Bongo would have his fingers in the logistics pot.

Operation Uhuru

For there is nothing covered, that shall not be revealed; neither hid, that shall not be known. Therefore whatsoever ye have spoken in darkness shall be heard in the light; and that which ye have spoken in the ear in closets shall be proclaimed upon the housetops.

—Gospel of Luke, XII

The Last Covert Action was christened Uhuru, Swahili for "freedom." The high-sounding objectives of the project were variations on familiar themes: supporting freedom and democracy, foiling Soviet subversion, and neutralizing the communist-supported PMFA.

The program had its genesis in Charleston, South Carolina, where arms, ammunition, and armored personnel carriers were loaded into the hold of a U.S. Victory ship. At the same time, forklifts loaded giant C-141 transport planes, their tailgates open like hungry mouths, with crates of M-16s, mortars, ammunition, and other supplies.

Paramilitary officers, many of them former colleagues from Southeast Asia operations, were rousted out on short notice and sent to Bintang. They stepped off the plane with tired and disbelieving eyes that asked why, so soon after Cham and Vietnam.

Technicians arrived with trunks full of pyrotechnic displays, demolition experts with suitcases crammed with plastic explosives, and an underwater demolition team (UDT) with limpets to blow open seams of Russian freighters. A special plane flew in loaded with portable printing presses and a mobile radio station. Last to arrive were the finance officers, their satchels stuffed with Portuguese escudos, Buwanan bank notes, and U.S. dollars to bankroll the FLA and UTIA and keep President Bongo's war chest replenished. Customs officials waved them all through, no questions asked.

To accommodate the influx of personnel, we went house hunting. There was a surplus of empty colonial villas, and their new Buwanan landlords were happy to accommodate dollar-paying tenants. A compound of four of these villas was leased for Uhuru's base of operations. The villas were soon furnished with desks, tables, chairs, and topographic sand tables. The walls of the briefing room were covered with maps and charts.

"Ft. Apache," with its clusters of roof antennas, wasn't hard to spot.

Heinzleman had made it clear he wanted "no smoking gun" in the Angafula operation. Uhuru was to be run as a covert operation, regardless of the large sums of money and number of personnel involved. Case officers had to be "sheep-dipped" (documented as foreign nationals) and weapons "sterilized" (non-U.S. origin). "Fig-leafed" covert actors had to perform on mobile operational stages, which could be easily dismantled if a press posse was spotted.

Sterilization and plausible denial. Good in theory, a nightmare to implement.

Uhuru had begun to take shape. The *American Chariot* docked at Katapi, and its cargo was immediately loaded onto freight cars lined up on a railroad spur. The railroad between Katapi and Bintang had deteriorated since the Belgians left in 1960, and it took three days instead of twelve hours to make the hundred-mile trip.

Outside Bintang the cargo was off-loaded from the train onto trucks and driven to an army quartermaster depot. The crates of M-16s, except for those set aside for the Presidential Guard, were turned over to the Buwanan army quartermaster to be exchanged for "sterile" fusils, bolt-action rifles that were standard issue for the Buwanan army.

It was hardly a fair exchange, and it almost spelled finis to Uhuru.

First, trying to hide the origin of the thousands of weapons in the hands of the FLA and UTIA was impractical, if not impossible. Angafula and Buwana were both leaky security sieves.

Also, the subterfuge was ill advised and unnecessary. M-16s could be bought on the black market anywhere in Africa or imported from Europe using doctored shipping manifests. Besides, since the Soviets were openly arming the PMFA with Russian Kalashnikovs, the submachine gun of choice of terrorists around the world, arming the FLA and UTIA with American M-16s shouldn't have raised any outcry.

Nevertheless, we had been ordered to turn over the new M-16s to the Buwanan quartermaster, who checked them off and then sent them by truck to a special warehouse guarded by Bongo's Presidential Guard. He then turned an equal number of their bolt-action rifles to the FLA and UTIA.

When Rebello and Sanchez saw the Buwanans carrying off shiny new M-16s and leaving rusty bolt-action rifles for the FLA and UTIA, the two leaders exploded. In a surprising show of unity, both began yelling at the Uhuru logistics officer, Tolbert. Rebello cried out that the fusils were so old and rusty and the barrels so pitted, they would either explode or backfire. Sanchez supported Rebello, yelling at Tolbert, "Give these rusting relics to those bastards in the PMFA so they'll blow up in their faces, not ours!"

Tolbert tried to calm the two incensed leaders, saying, "*Faites-moi confiance!* Trust me!"

I knew something had gone wrong when the easygoing Tolbert burst into my office and started banging on my desk and said, "*Quel bordel!* A real cock-up! Uhuru is about to go down the tubes with this stupid shell game of switching new M-16s for rusted Belgian muskets. We might as well give them muzzle loaders and be done with it! I told Rebello and Sanchez I'd talk to you about stopping this 'castration, sterilization,' or whatever you want to call it. Both of them are so steamed up they are ready to say to hell with Uhuru unless something is done to that farce out at the warehouse!"

Uhuru was foundering before it even got started. I asked Tolbert to sit down and together we would draft a message requesting a waiver in the Uhuru weapons sterilization requirement and ask for authorization to issue the M-16s directly to Rebello and Sanchez or their representatives, pointing out that the Soviets were arming the PMFA with Kalashnikovs. Issuing M-16s to the FLA and UTIA would level the playing field.

Bongo would obviously not be happy with the change, and we recommended offering him fifty M-16s for his presidential honor guard in Ladolite, the location of his summer palace, and a "slush fund" for the quartermaster and his crew.

Headquarters must have done some arm-twisting, because within twenty-four hours, "sterilization" had been excised from the Uhuru lexicon. Bongo protested the change as predicted but came around with the sweetener of the M-16s for his honor guard.

"Sterilization" and "plausible denial" had taken a hit, but Uhuru was back on track.

Stark

Stark's qualification for coordinating the task force was that he had spent part of his childhood in Africa as the son of missionary parents and had a smattering of Swahili, a language spoken in a remote corner of Angafula.

When Stark arrived in my office, he was wearing a black safari suit and black boots. A silver Maltese cross dangled from his neck, glinting as he introduced himself and asked for immediate transportation to "the front." I arranged for a chartered Air Buwana Fokker to take him to Rebello's headquarters in Ambrizio and later on to Sanchez's base in the interior. I told Stark the plane would pick him up when he was ready to return to Bintang.

Two weeks after he left, Stark was back in my office. His safari suit was still unrumpled and spotless. He handed me the report he had prepared for the task force and an envelope containing Polaroid snapshots of his trip. I looked at the snapshots: Stark and Rebello standing next to a bullet-riddled sign pointing toward Lunda; Stark standing with Sanchez on top of a burned-out half-track, the red PMFA star still visible; Stark looking at PMFA prisoners; and Stark talking to UTIA guerrillas.

Stark said he had been impressed by both Rebello and Sanchez. He was convinced that with additional training and weapons, their combined forces would soon control most of Angafula. He said it was all in his report, and he would appreciate being able to add my comments.

I hastily read the report and then handed it back to Stark. I said I wouldn't add any comments because the report was Stark's personal assessment and should stand on its own. I did say that I found his report somewhat optimistic, probably because it hadn't taken into account the African Equation. Stark looked puzzled, and I explained.

As Stark was aware, Africa was unfathomable and unpredictable. Elephant droppings and tribal drumbeats were as reliable in predicting the future as intelligence estimates and projections. Angafula was a witches' brew that was currently being stirred by tribal shamans, village chiefs, guerrillas, and foreign interlopers. The brew was simmering but one day it would boil over.

For the first time Stark stopped fingering his Maltese cross. He was probably wondering whether I was pulling his leg with African mumbo jumbo.

He reached over and took back his report, and the following day he left for Washington.

In fairness to Stark, he didn't know the cauldron was about to boil over, and when it did, ten thousand Cuban volunteers spilled out—and rendered his report worthless.

The Flying Circus

Je vous querir un grand peut-etre,
irez le rideau, la farce est jouee.

—FRANÇOIS RABELAIS

Supplying Uhuru forces inside Angafula was dangerous and difficult. It was pointless to ferry supplies across the river because there were no roads on the other side to truck them into the interior. Portaging the heavy crates for long treks through the jungle was impractical, slow, and dangerous. As a result, crates of supplies from the *American Chariot* were stacked in Bintang warehouses. Supplies flown in by C-141 and C-130 cargo planes had to be off-loaded in Bintang because American aircraft were forbidden to fly into Angafulan air space.

Uhuru desperately needed an air bridge into Angafula. We had tried chartering Air Buwana planes, but the airline was unreliable, with crews showing up late or not at all, and the planes frequently down for repairs, hors de service, for weeks at a time. The supply pipeline had slowed to a trickle, and the project was grinding to a halt.

Then fortune smiled on Uhuru.

With Angafula drifting into civil war, Portuguese expatriates began leaving the country. When a leftist government came to power in Lisbon and announced its support for Sappho's PMFA, more Portuguese joined the exodus out of Angafula. Some Portuguese, however remained in Angafula, and from among these emerged Uhuru's first foreign "volunteers."

Obie, the Uhuru air operations officer, woke me at midnight. An Air Angafula plane with a Portuguese crew had landed at Bintang's international airport. Obie said the pilot was waiting outside. I told Obie to bring the pilot in and offered him a cold beer before asking him to sit down and tell us his story.

Carlos said he was a Fokker pilot for Air Angafula, the Portuguese charter airline serving the colony. Carlos had filed a flight plan in Lunda for Carmona, a regular destination. The tower cleared his flight, and Carlos took off, but about fifty kilometers north of Lunda, he altered course for Buwana. Approaching Bintang, Carlos radioed the tower, requesting permission to land. The flight was unscheduled, but the tower operator authorized the plane to land, ordering Carlos to taxi to an unmarked hangar at the far end of the runway.

When the plane taxied up to the hangar, one of the guards immediately called Obie, who instructed the guard to open the hangar and have the pilot park the plane inside. Obie had immediately gone out to the airport and talked to Captain Carlos. The two men had then come directly to my house.

Carlos's story was that he had heard on the Portuguese grapevine that the Americans were supporting Angafula anticommunist movements. Carlos and his

crew were fed up with the leftist colonial government in Lunda and had decided
to come to Bintang to offer their services.

Leaving Carlos to nurse his beer, Obie and I went into my study, where we
discussed the various options open to us regarding the Air Angafula plane and its
crew and finally narrowed them down to three: The first option was to turn the
crew and plane over to the Buwanans. This wouldn't endear us to the Buwanan
Security Service, which would not want to get its president involved in a diplomatic row with a foreign government. The second option was to notify the
Portuguese embassy. The Portuguese ambassador would immediately inform his
government and demand that the Buwanan authorities impound the plane and
send the crew to Lunda to face charges. This was another course of action that
would not sit well with President Bongo, who had little use for the Portuguese
and would have to resist any attempts at extradition, but would not like getting
involved. The third option, and the one we settled on, was to hide the plane, stash
the crew, and then decide on a plan of action. Obie said he already had a plan. All
he needed to implement it was a special hangar, plenty of paint, a few technicians,
and approval to put Captain Carlos and his crew on the Uhuru payroll.

When Obie advised Carlos, the pilot thanked him on behalf of all the crew. He
said more "volunteers" would come soon, which was borne out when a second
Air Angafula plane arrived the following week. The third plane landed three days
later, the last "defector" plane before the Portuguese authorities grounded the rest
of the Air Angafula fleet.

Air piracy protests, lodged by the Portuguese ambassador with the Foreign
Ministry, were "duly noted" and filed away. Obie drew up an official-looking
document incorporating Peter Pan Airlines, signed at the bottom by James Barrie,
president.

The first freshly painted "Peter Pan" Fokker with a new tail number and
redocumented crew emerged from Obie's hangar in less than a month. Along with
the two other planes, which joined the fleet soon afterward, the charter airline
began flying supplies into Angafula, and before long the warehouse had almost
been emptied of the backlog of supplies.

Uhuru finally had its air bridge.

Mister Brown

The Portuguese ambassador was not the only one upset about the pirated
Fokkers. Ralph Brown, the U.S. Federal Aviation Administration (FAA) adviser
at Njili Airport, had become increasingly curious about the activity at the "special
hangar." He decided to go see for himself what Obie was up to.

Brown had met Obie, but the two men had never gotten along, Brown resenting the rapport the Apaloosa horse breeder from New Mexico had with Buwanan airport officials. Obie, for his part, had little use for the FAA technocrat.

One day Brown walked down to the special hangar and saw Buwanans stenciling a new number on the tail of a freshly painted Fokker. He stomped into Obie's office in the back of the hangar: "Obie, you must be crazy! You can't change tail numbers on a plane like license plates on a car! Those tail numbers are internationally registered. Altering them is a violation of international law! I'm going to report you to the FAA!"

Obie looked up at the fuming Brown, surprised to see the normally taciturn FAA adviser so excited. He got up out of his chair and walked around his desk, putting his hand on Brown's shoulder. "It's OK, Ralph, don't sweat it! National security operation; know what I mean?"

Brown shook off Obie's hand, turned, and stormed out of the office repeating his threat to report Obie to the proper authorities.

Brown was eventually called back to Washington for "medical consultations," which Obie attributed to "hallucinations of tail numbers dancing in his head."

The MiGs

> Yet much is oft in the course of deeds that move the wheels of the world: small hands do them because they must, while the eyes of the great are elsewhere.
>
> —J. R. R. TOLKIEN, *Lord of the Rings*

Obie's airlift was going full steam. Repainted planes took off before their new colors had time to dry. If there were a place for air operations in the *Guinness Book of World Records*, Obie's would have been right behind the Berlin airlift.

For one urgent flight to Sanchez's base in the interior, however, he had to charter an Air Buwana Fokker with an American crew. The plane was to make a stop for a load of rations in a neighboring country to avoid paying the exorbitant surcharges levied by Bongo's Bintang vendors and to pick up a French TV cameraman contracted by Sanchez to film a documentary about UTIA.

Sanchez was waiting at the airstrip when the plane landed and invited the crew and cameraman to join him at his command post next to the airstrip while the rations were being unloaded. Two planes suddenly appeared overhead. Sanchez's troops unloading the rations stopped to wave at the planes, assuming they were friendly Cessnas that occasionally flew reconnaissance missions for UTIA. This time, however, the planes were not friendly Cessnas. They dove down toward the airstrip, rockets spewing from their wings. The American pilot recognized the silhouette of the planes and yelled out, "Take cover! They're MiGs!"

Sanchez also began shouting, "MiGs! *Ce sont les MiGs! Planquez-vous!* Get down, they're MiGs!"

The two MiGs roared down over the airstrip, their rockets kicking up clouds of dust as they screeched along the airstrip toward the Fokker. One of the rockets skewed off the runway, but the second one hit the Fokker behind the cockpit. By this time the TV cameraman was on his feet filming the attack and shouting epithets at the Russian "swine" when the MiG's streaked past. The MiGs then circled back to make another pass. On the second sortie, a rocket scored a direct hit on the Fokker's fuel tank, setting the plane on fire. The MiGs pulled up and circled over the airstrip, wagging their wings as they made a final pass en route back to Lunda.

The covert war had burst from its cocoon

—⁂—

After the MiG attack, Sanchez decided to move his base farther into the interior. He sent a squad of his soldiers to escort the Fokker crew and the cameraman through the jungle to Bintang. They arrived two weeks later, with the TV film still intact.

The TV film was made into a documentary in Europe, and a copy was sent to Headquarters. The film of the MiG attack was evidence of Soviet intervention in Angafula, and I was certain it could be used to counter critics of American involvement. The decision was made, however, that the film raised too many questions. Who had provided the plane to bring in rations to Sanchez, the Air Buwana logo still visible on the tail of the charred wreckage? Who had provided the foreign rations still scattered around the airstrip?

Even though the planes were MiGs, the Russians would deny any involvement, claiming the MiGs were part of the Angafulan air force and the pilots were Cuban volunteers.

A covert standoff. The MiGs canceled out the *American Chariot.*

The film went into the archives at Langley. After the loss of his plane in the MiG attack, President Bongo demanded two million dollars to replace the Fokker. He reluctantly accepted a hundred and fifty thousand dollars, the going price of a used Fokker on a lot in Texas.

On the Ground

The war was heating up, and the FLA was going on the offensive. Rebello had recently acquired two foreign military advisers, Colonel Joao Castillo and

Captain Luis Bentavo. Castillo, a former Portuguese army colonel, was short, bald, and carried a swagger stick, a martinet of the old school. Bentavo, an ex-captain in Brazil's special forces, was stocky and muscular. A jagged scar ran down his left cheek.

Castillo and Bentavo went with me on one of my visits to Rebello's FLA base in Ambrizio.

Ambrizio is a small fishing village on the Atlantic about twenty miles north of Lunda. Gentle swells lap at pirogues laying on the beach next to the fishing nets splayed in the sun. The town square is lined with coconut palms shading an Evangelical church with empty teakwood pews. In the cemetery behind the church, bleached teak crosses mark the graves of three shipwrecked American seamen.

Rebello's driver was waiting at the airstrip north of Ambrizio. We had just climbed into the jeep and driven off when two planes appeared overhead. The driver slammed on the brakes, and we scrambled out of the jeep, diving for cover. I thought the MiGs were staging a repeat performance, but when I looked up from the ditch, I saw Castillo and Bentavo standing nearby, waving at the planes, which flew off wagging their wings. Bentavo came over and told me they were Portuguese air force planes flying reconnaissance for the PMFA. He and Castillo had recognized the pilots, who were old friends, adding they wouldn't report having seen us when they returned to Lunda.

It was becoming harder to tell friend from foe.

Rebello's headquarters was in a former schoolhouse. He was standing in front of a map when we arrived, and after a cursory greeting, he began his briefing. He pointed to a line of green arrows on the map, which he said indicated recent FLA advances. He then moved his pointer to Lunda, the capital of Angafula. The capital was circled in red.

"Two weeks from today my forces will be in Lunda, having driven out the PMFA. Lunda is our first objective. After we have taken the capital, we will move south and capture Caxico, where the PMFA has a large base. This will give us complete control of western Angafula."

It was a grand plan, but I noticed Castillo hadn't reacted. The ex-colonel remained stone-faced, and Bentavo, who had crushed out his cigarette, sat staring at the ceiling. The two military men were unimpressed by the grandiose plan of the religious mystic standing in front of them.

Without commenting on his briefing, Castillo stood up and asked Rebello to take us to the FLA command post (CP). I saw that Rebello was crestfallen, because his two new advisers had dismissed his plan out of hand. We all got in his jeep and drove up to the CP.

The CP was on a knoll overlooking the Kwanza River. The sun had just gone down, and off to the south in the distance we could make out lights flickering on.

The lights marked the outskirts of Lunda. Pointing to the lights, Rebello again brought up his plan for capturing the capital. He was immediately cut off by Castillo, who berated Rebello for being naive, unrealistic, and overconfident. He told the FLA leader his forces would be lucky to advance two or three miles down the road before being cut down by the PMFA, which would have set up ambushes and planted land mines. The PMFA, with their superior force, would counterattack and probably drive the FLA into the sea.

Rebello shifted uneasily. When Castillo finished, Rebello told the colonel he had a "surprise" to show him that might change his mind and led us down a path to a clearing. A group of men in camouflage uniforms were standing around a fire. One of them stepped out to greet Rebello, who immediately introduced us to Colonel Piet, his "artillery adviser." Colonel Piet spoke English with a Dutch accent that indicated he probably came from a country further south.

Prompted by Rebello, Colonel Piet pointed to two 105-mm howitzers under camouflage nets. The two howitzers were pointed toward Lunda, and I understood why Rebello had seemed so confident back in Ambrizio. The two 105s would provide artillery support for his march on Lunda, and even Castillo and Bentavo seemed impressed by this surprise addition to the FLA. With two 105s to back up their offensive, Rebello's FLA might take Lunda after all.

Rebello's plan might have succeeded, if the PMFA hadn't come up with a "surprise" of its own. Rebello's forces had advanced less than three kilometers toward Lunda when they suddenly came under a withering rocket barrage. In less than an hour, the heralded FLA advance to Lunda suddenly turned into a disorganized rout.

105-mm howitzers versus multiple-rocket launchers. The war was, as Alice had said, becoming "curiouser and curiouser."

On the Sea

Before the advent of Uhuru, I had been invited by John, an English friend, and his Portuguese partner, Sebastian, to visit their tuna processing plant in Angafula on the Atlantic coast sixty miles south of Lunda. The plant was new and was equipped with modern machinery and the latest in cold storage refrigeration. After they took me on a tour of their plant, we went out on one of their fishing trawlers, sailing down the coast as far as the port of Iguano.

Six months after my visit, the PMFA attacked the "capitalist" tuna processing plant and destroyed most of the machinery. John and Sebastian escaped on the newest of their trawlers, the *Christina*, the two older trawlers, the *Pilar* and the *Santa Lucia*, following in the *Christina*'s wake. Three days later the fishing fleet pulled into the Buwanan port of Hatapi, where, after paying hefty "landing fees" to local harbor officials, they were granted asylum.

They had been in Katapi for several weeks when John and Sebastian began to feel uneasy. The local fishermen had begun eyeing their trawlers, which were bigger and more modern than Buwanan fishing boats. The two men had wanted to sell their trawlers but were now worried that the boats would be plundered before they could find a buyer. They had heard about Uhuru through the Portuguese grapevine and came to see me in Bintang to inquire if the American embassy could use some fishing boats.

I hadn't thought about an Uhuru maritime capability, but since some of our land offensives weren't doing too well, I decided a sea option was worth considering. I remembered the World War Q-boats, merchant ships with concealed cannons preying on vulnerable cargo vessels. Why not armed Uhuru trawlers flying the Jolly Roger to prey on Soviet ships supplying UTIA?

Getting back to reality, John proposed offering Bongo two of the fishing trawlers, the *Pilar* and the *Santa Lucia*, in exchange for guaranteeing the security of the *Christina*. The *Christina* would be leased to an unnamed American fishing company.

It was a good plan. The two trawlers would be profitable additions to the Buwanan fishing fleet in Katapi, and with their catch, could help feed the local population and Buwanan troops. Uhuru had no maritime assets, and Angafula's coastline and harbors presented a number of tempting targets. Soviet ships were frequently docking in Lunda with munitions and supplies for the PMFA. There were also several PMFA bases along the coast, bases vulnerable to attacks from the sea.

The *Christina* would add a new dimension to Uhuru.

When I met with Bongo, he was enthusiastic about the addition of two free trawlers to his fishing fleet and immediately gave orders to the naval commander in Bintang to ensure the security of the *Christina*.

Uhuru now had a maritime capability.

Tom Maree, known to colleagues as the "old seadog," was already in Katapi offering training to Buwanan crews on the operation of the two new Swift boats the Buwanans had on loan to provide security for the presidential yacht, the *Anne Marie*.

Swift boats were not new to Buwana, two of them having been shipped over piecemeal to assist in the pursuit of Che Guevara, the Argentine revolutionary who was stirring up trouble in the Lakes Region. The Buwanans had pursued the elusive bandito for several months, until finally the two Swift boats disappeared without a trace.

The "old seadog" never got the chance to train the Buwanan crews. The officer in charge said they didn't need any training or instructions on the maintenance of the boats and insisted Maree turn over the keys. We learned afterward that the Swifts were never used as planned to provide security for the presidential yacht. They were mostly taken out and used by Bongo's ministers and generals for fishing excursions and chasing crocodiles. Eventually, both Swifts had to be beached for lack of maintenance.

I asked Maree to check out the *Christina*. He reported back that the trawler was in good condition and could easily be converted for use in maritime operations. He recommended bolting a gyroscopic mortar on the forward deck and acquiring a fast powerboat to provide security for the slower trawler. A Gatling gun and grenade launcher to ward off any pursuers should be installed on the power boat.

I asked Sebastian if he knew where I could get a powerboat. He knew just the place: the Lunda Yacht Club.

As the security situation in Lunda deteriorated, yacht club members put their boats up for sale. Escudos or dollars, no questions asked. Sebastian sent a message to his cousin, a member of the yacht club board of directors, advising him that two "friends" would be coming to Lunda to purchase a twin-engine powerboat. He asked his cousin to help them find what they needed.

Jack Torrance, a maritime expert, and Ernesto de Silva, his Portuguese interpreter, were provided with fake Brazilian passports for the trip to Lunda. They stashed an air-to-sea radio in the false bottom of one of their suitcases and packets of dollars and escudos in the other.

When they arrived in Lunda, they took the only available taxi to the yacht club, where Pinto's cousin, Alonzo, was waiting in his office. Once Alonzo satisfied himself that the two men were Pinto's bona fide friends, he went down with them to the boat slips. There were a number of powerboats for sale, from small runabouts to luxurious yachts. Torrance settled on the *De Gama*, a red-and-white Chris-Craft with twin eighty-horsepower Mercury engines. They then returned to Alonzo's office, where they paid for the boat and signed a bill of sale. Alonzo gave them two fishing rods and a picnic basket packed with sandwiches and a bottle of Portuguese wine. Looking around to make sure no one was watching, Alonzo lifted the napkins covering the sandwiches. Two smoke grenades had been stashed on the bottom of the basket.

The new owners of the *De Gama* returned to the slip, gassed up the tanks and auxiliaries, and cast off, pointing the *De Gama* toward the outer islands. In less than an hour, the *De Gama* was skimming alongside the barrier reef ringing the islands. Torrance throttled back the engines so Ernesto could begin trolling off the back of the boat. Torrance took out the sea-to-air radio to contact Obie's Beechraft, which was flying surveillance for the operation. On Torrance's second try, the pilot answered, saying he had the *De Gama* in sight and advised Torrance to swing the boat around and head north toward Matadi.

Ten minutes later the pilot radioed that he had spotted an armed patrol boat leaving Lunda harbor heading in the direction of the *De Gama*. Torrance throttled the engines forward and yelled at Ernesto to get out the smoke grenades.

The patrol boat came up fast and was gaining on the *De Gama* when Ernesto pulled the pin on one of the grenades and threw it off the stern. The trail of white smoke from the grenade shielded the *De Gama* temporarily from its pursuers, but a short time later the patrol boat reappeared. Ernesto then threw a second grenade, and Torrance pushed the throttle "full ahead." The bow of the *De Gama* rose up in the air, and Ernesto grabbed onto the gunwale to keep from falling overboard.

Several minutes later they looked back. The patrol boat had given up the chase and was heading back to Lunda. Torrance eased off the throttle, and the *De Gama* resumed heading north. Two hours later, they reached the port of Katapi, The *De Gama* pulled in and docked alongside its new mother ship, the *Christina*.

Soldiers of Fortune

These, in the day when heaven was falling,
The hour when earth's foundations fled,
Followed their mercenary calling,
And took their wages, and are dead.
—A. E. HOUSMAN, "Epitaph on an Army of Mercenaries"

Bongo had once told Rebello that mercenaries had been the key to his rise to power. His stories about "Major Mike"—Mike Hoare, a famous mercenary in Africa—had not been lost on Rebello, whose forces had recently taken a beating and were being pressed hard near Ambrizio.

Former Lance Corporal Cullen, accompanied by two bodyguards, arrived at my house around midnight asking if he could "have a word." The crew cuts and stiff bearing of the three men gave away their military background. Suspecting they were mercenaries, I asked them to leave, but Cullen wouldn't budge. He insisted on my hearing him out and promised to be brief. Reluctantly, I relented and let the three men inside.

Inside the house, Cullen removed a .45 caliber pistol from his jacket. He laid the pistol on a table with the comment that it "it wasn't good form" to wear a sidearm in a host's home. I motioned for the visitors to sit down, but only Cullen took me up on the offer. The other two men remained standing.

Cullen's slate-gray eyes matched the barrel of his pistol. They kept darting around the room until they finally locked in on his host. His ramrod posture and steely countenance made me uneasy. At the same time, he had my full attention.

Cullen said he and the others had answered an ad in a London newspaper seeking "soldiers of fortune" to fight in Africa. The ad, which I later learned had been placed by Rebello's cousin, the FLA representative in London, guaranteed selected applicants good pay and a $10,000 recruitment bonus.

Thirteen applicants, an ominous number as it turned out, were selected and given plane tickets to Bintang, Buwana. They would receive the $10,000 bonus in Bintang from FLA president, Rebello.

When the mercenaries arrived in Buwana, no one from the FLA was at the airport to meet them. Rebello's cousin had given Cullen, the self-appointed leader of the group, my name and address. Cullen had decided to seek me out to get directions to FLA headquarters.

I tried to keep my anger at Rebello from showing. I was furious that Rebello had given my name and address to his cousin, who in turn had given it to a mercenary. I had warned Rebello when he brought the subject up to have nothing to do with mercenaries, that using "hired guns" would taint the FLA and discredit him as its leader. I had also stressed that it was Agency policy to have nothing to do with mercenaries, and by going behind my back, he had not only made me vulnerable, but also had poisoned the well for Uhuru.

I would deal with Rebello later. The immediate problem was the mercenaries in my house. In a way, I sympathized with their plight. They had been blindsided in London by a fraudulent ad promising them high pay and a bonus they would probably never receive. They hadn't been told anything about the operation they had signed on for that would most likely, in the end, leave them broke, maimed, and probably dead.

I told Cullen I couldn't help him. Having any contact with mercenaries was forbidden, and I had made an exception in letting them in. However, since they were here, I would offer them some advice. I told them to go back to the airport and take the next plane for London. If they stayed and ended up in Angafula fighting for the FLA, they would probably not get paid, they would never see their bonus, and there was a good chance they would never return home.

I waited for a reaction and wasn't surprised when there wasn't any. Cullen merely nodded, saying they had made a commitment, which they would honor. Cullen said he himself had served in the British army and had fought more than two years against Chinese communist guerrillas in the jungles of Malaysia. Angafula couldn't be that much different.

I asked Cullen and his bodyguards to come into my study. Unrolling a map of Angafula and spreading it out on my desk, I indicated the "unfriendly" areas, controlled by the PMFA. I then showed them the FLA forward base at Ambrizio, where Rebello would probably send them, tracing the treacherous route from FLA headquarters to the coast.

I told Cullen he and his men would get little support once they left the FLA's base in Bintang. If they ran into trouble, the FLA wouldn't be able to support them. Rebello would issue the group rations, arms, and some ammunition and would probably provide them with an FLA escort. But Cullen and his men would basically be on their own. Cullen should also realize that Rebello's headquarters was penetrated by the PMFA. Their spies would immediately report the departure of Cullen and his group for Ambrizio.

On their way to Ambrizio, they would encounter PMFA patrols and ambushes. When the first shots were fired, his FLA escort would disappear, leaving Cullen and his group on their own. In addition to ambushes and firefights, they would be up against wild animals, poisonous vipers, and crocodiles, and his men would come down with dengue fever, malaria, heat exhaustion, and the green monkey disease.

Cullen's expression didn't change. He seemed unperturbed by my stark portrayal of the dangers facing him and his men.

When I finished the briefing, I rolled up the map and brought out three cold beers, and a half hour later they left. Cullen thanked me for the briefing and the beer and said he would not reveal having met me or been to my house.

I told my sentinel to escort them to Rebello's headquarters.

I never saw Cullen again.

A Fatal Journey

And so, if I take the journey
I fear it might turn out an act of folly.
—DANTE ALIGHERI, *Inferno*

Cullen and his group never made it to Ambrizio. Two weeks after they had left Rebello's headquarters, they had made it only halfway to the coast. By that time the group was down to ten from the original thirteen. Two had been killed in an ambush; one died from malaria.

Rebello's escort, as I had warned Cullen, had deserted during the first firefight, leaving the group to fend for itself. With their rations almost gone, the remaining mercenaries, except for Cullen, wanted to go back. When the ex-corporal ordered them to keep going, they mutinied. Cullen shot two of the mutineers and ordered the others to bury them. He then forced the remainder of his column to push on.

The group was ambushed again and this time overpowered and taken prisoner. They were force-marched to Lunda and tried as spies.

With the exception of Cullen, the mercenaries all signed confessions admitting to being "CIA spies" and were sentenced to twenty years of hard labor. Cullen remained defiant, insisting to the end that he was a soldier and not a spy. He was executed by a firing squad in Lunda's main square.

True to his promise, Cullen, although tortured and beaten, never revealed having contacted me in Bintang.

A year after I had returned from Buwana, I was contacted by a London lawyer representing Cullen's widow. He told me Cullen had told his wife before leaving England that he was going to Angafula "on a special mission for the CIA." When Mrs. Cullen heard he had been executed in Lunda, she contacted the Agency about his death benefits and was advised there was no record of her husband having been employed by the Agency.

Mrs. Cullen was later visited by a former member of Cullen's group, who had been released from prison in Angafula as part of a special amnesty. He told her about the meeting at my house in Bintang before they left on their ill-fated journey.

Reinforced in her conviction that her husband had been working for the Agency, she asked a lawyer friend if he would try to contact me and support her claim that her husband had worked for the Agency. According to the lawyer, she was desperate, having two children to support and no money.

I told the lawyer I felt sorry for Mrs. Cullen, but I reiterated that her husband had no association with the Agency. I admitted, off the record, that Cullen had come to see me and that I had warned him not to get involved with the FLA. I laid out for him the risks and dangers of going to Angafula and urged him in the strongest terms to return to England. Cullen however, believed he had a commitment to fulfill and refused to take my advice. I added that, as the lawyer was probably aware, Cullen never admitted to any association with the Agency even when tortured and threatened with execution.

The lawyer told me he realized Mrs. Cullen was not entitled to any compensation from the Agency. He wondered however if there was anything I could do "unofficially" to help Cullen's widow.

I replied, again off the record, that I would make inquiries of a British military friend if he had any idea how to help the widow of a former soldier in Her Majesty's service.

Several months later, the lawyer called me from London. He had heard that Mrs. Cullen had been granted a war-widow's pension by the British government.

Mrs. Cullen, like others, will have to cling to the covert shroud surrounding her husband's death, convinced he died in a noble cause.

Stalin's Organs and the Cubans

Her plot hath many changes; every day speaks a new scene.
—FRANCIS QUARLES, "Epigram: Respice Fenim"

The Soviets had no intention of allowing Uhuru to upset their plans for Angafula. The MiGs had been a harbinger.

Rebello sent another urgent message asking me to come to Ambrizio. The idyllic town had frayed since our last visit. Fruit and fish vendors' stalls were bare, the marketplace was deserted, the church boarded up. Rust was inching up the turrets of the half-track panhards in front of Rebello's headquarters.

As for Robello, I hardly recognized the Saladin firebrand of a few weeks before, chafing to march on Lunda. His pallor was ashen, his cheeks were sunken, and the wrinkles in his forehead seemed to have deepened. The ill-fated march on Lunda had taken its toll, and for the first time I felt sorry for the FLA leader.

We rode to his forward command post, now less than five kilometers from Ambrizio. As the front receded, Colonel Piet had moved his howitzers further to the rear, and his crews were busy digging foxholes and piling sandbags around freshly dug revetments. Colonel Piet came over and handed me a piece of shrapnel. "Souvenir from a 'Stalin's Organ.' Sappho now has a Russian toy in his arsenal."

Stalin's Organs, truck-mounted, six-tube, 122-mm rocket launchers, played a key role in the defense of Stalingrad in World War II. Their appearance in Angafula was an ominous sign. An even more ominous escalation in the form of foreign volunteers would follow.

When we returned to Ambrizio, Rebello had another surprise in store for us. Standing in front of the same map he had used to brief us on the abortive Lunda operation, the green arrows pointing from Ambrizio to the capital had been rubbed out. A new line of boat-shaped arrows on the sea pointed toward Lunda.

Rebello tapped his pointer on the line of boats. He said his agents had reported that two ships had landed in Lunda and debarked more than two thousand Cuban troops from the Fidel Castro brigade. The Cuban "volunteers" had been sent directly to the front to reinforce PMFA forces sent to repel FLA troops advancing toward Ambrizio. Rebello's forces had suddenly come under attack from battalions of Cuban regulars supported by Soviet rocket launchers and had been forced to withdraw.

I had to hand it to the FLA leader. His vaunted march on Lunda had turned into a rout, his entire front was collapsing, and he stood there blaming it all on battalions of Cubans and Stalin's Organs.

We already had confirmation of the Stalin's Organs from Piet, but the Cuban intervention was too far-fetched, particularly because Rebello's "agents" were mostly low-level informants whose reports were concoctions of rumor and gossip. If Cuban troops had been sent from Havana to Angafula, Headquarters would have alerted the Station. Holden was crying wolf to divert attention from the recent rout of his troops during their ill-fated march to Lunda.

Unfortunately for Uhuru, Rebello had not been crying wolf. When I returned to Bintang, a cable was on my desk confirming the departure from Havana of two ships carrying twenty-five hundred troops from the elite Fidel Castro brigade. The message also confirmed their arrival in Lunda.

I had to eat crow and apologize to Rebello.

Stalin's Organs and the intervention of Cuban "volunteers." The covert war was spinning out of control.

The Long Round

The real success . . . in frightening [the enemy was] the sound of fired cannon [which] sent every man within earshot behind cover. They thought weapons destructive in proportion to their noise [and] their moral confidence was to be restored only by having guns, useful or useless, but noisy, on their side . . . artillery, artillery, artillery.

—T. E. LAWRENCE, *Seven Pillars of Wisdom*

President Bongo was angry. Recent reverses in Angafula had not set well with the president, and he sent for me. When I arrived, he was talking to his chief of staff, General Bumba. A young artillery captain stood next to him. The president turned and wagged his finger at me and said, "Mr. St. Martin, why are you standing by while the Russians supply the PMFA with Orgues de Stalin? Why do you allow them to outgun our FLA friends? Why can't you supply Rebello with big guns like 155s so he can fight back?"

The president didn't wait for me to answer, which was fortunate, because I didn't have a good answer.

"Since you won't do anything to stop the Cubans and their Stalin's Organs, I will!" he continued. "Two years ago the North Koreans gave us two long-range 140-mm cannons. When I expelled the North Koreans later, I didn't give them back their cannons. Those cannons have a range of thirty-five kilometers, which is more than enough to reach Lunda from Ambrizio!"

He waited for this revelation to sink in, and then he went on. "Tomorrow I am sending my artillery officer, Captain Ilongo, to Ambrizio with the two North Korean cannons. When he gets them set up and begins shelling Lunda with these 140-mm cannons, the Cubans will run all the way back to Havana! I want you to go with Captain Ilongo to Ambrizio so you can see for yourself my big guns in action. Then *you* can report to Washington what *we* do to help our friends when they're in trouble!"

The president was pleased with himself. He squared his leopard-skin toque and left with General Bumba. Captain Ilongo, who had been smiling and nodding while Bongo was speaking, remained behind.

After Bongo left, I saw that the young artillery captain was no longer smiling. He confided to me that he was worried. He hadn't wanted to say anything, but he didn't dare tell the president about the guns. He said that when the North Koreans left, they took all the firing tables for the 140-mm cannons with them. The distressed captain said it hadn't mattered until now. They rolled the cannons out only once a year, towing them down Boulevard Bongo for the Independence Day parade. The two guns had never even been fired.

I understood why Ilongo was nervous. Without firing tables, there was no way of knowing the amount of powder and propellant to pack into the breech for the "maximum charge" required for the shells to hit Lunda. It was like trying to bake a cake without a recipe.

Ilongo asked if there was any way I could get him a 140-mm firing table, maybe from my military friends. I told Ilongo I would try, and I did. Unfortunately, by the time a firing table was found, Ilongo and I were on our way to Ambrizio.

The two big cannons rolled down the ramp from the rear of a Buwana air force C-130. Trucks were standing by on the tarmac to tow them to the front, where the cannons were unhooked and wheeled into place behind newly prepared revetments. Ilongo's crews climbed onto the big guns and swiveled the long barrels around until they pointed toward Lunda. The two ironclad behemoths, poking their long snouts over the elephant grass, looked like mammoth Jurassic Park anteaters.

Captain Ilongo paced back and forth, glancing over to see if by some miracle I had come up with a firing table. When he decided he couldn't wait any longer, he ordered "maximum charge" to the crew of the first cannon. When the charge had been packed into the breech, he gave the order to fire. The crew chief pulled the lanyard, and the big gun roared, bucked into the air, and exploded. Reverberations from the blast threw everyone to the ground. No one moved as the debris rained down over the area.

When the cloud of yellow smoke finally lifted, the carnage around what was left of the big cannon became visible. It was a gruesome sight. The remains of the crew and the gun sergeant, the lanyard still clutched in his hand, were splattered around the revetment. Captain Ilongo, his head partially severed from his body, was barely recognizable. A long gash ran down along the barrel of the cannon, which lay on its side, with one wheel still spinning in the air. Molten fragments, some still glowing, were scattered over the area.

We went out to cover the remains of Ilongo and his crew. The carcass of the cannon, wisps of smoke still curling from its serrated barrel, was dragged down to the beach.

Wally, a psychological warfare officer stationed in Ambrizio, arrived a short time later carrying a bottle of Four Roses. He proposed a toast "To Captain Ilongo and his crew, may their names be forever inscribed on that Uhuru headstone in the sky!" Local legend has it that the "long round" kept orbiting over Lunda until the Cubans left Angafula. It then dove into the ocean, resurfaced with newly sprouted fins, and guided the convoy back to Havana.

The entry of the Cubans added a new dimension to the covert war. The FLA and UTIA irregulars were no match for the battalions of Fidel's finest. Their hit-and-run sabotage operations and commando raids against the PMFA and their Cuban allies were pinpricks against a formidable foe.

Some psychological warfare operations were more successful.

Wally

Like the catastrophe of the old comedy.
My cue is villainous melancholy,
with a sigh like Tom o'Bedlam.
—W. SHAKESPEARE, *King Lear*

Wally had spent fifteen years grinding out propaganda for a number of Agency programs. He had tried without success for an overseas assignment and had never been able to break away from Headquarters. When Wally heard about Operation Uhuru, he immediately volunteered. His request was again turned down because he was "badly needed at Headquarters." But this time the angry and frustrated Wally threatened to resign and take his talents to Proctor and Gamble, where they would be more appreciated. Headquarters relented, and Wally was sent out to run Uhuru's agitprop program.

Wally set up shop in Ambrizio, and several weeks after his arrival Radio Free Angafula (RFA) came on the air broadcasting in three tribal dialects. The radio offered PMFA soldiers amnesty if they gave themselves up and joined UTIA or the FLA.

He also set up a parallel "black" radio supposedly broadcasting from Havana. Radio Havana warned Cuban soldiers to beware of the PMFA's pleasure women camp infected with the incurable Sappho venereal disease. Radio Havana also urged Cuban volunteers to desert and smuggle themselves back to Havana to protect their wives from KGB predators.

One evening when Wally was out walking, a rocket slammed into his radio shack. Unperturbed, the next day Wally flew to Bintang and spent several days scrounging Le Cite's black markets until he found a secondhand transmitter. Within a week Radio Angafula was back on the air.

During lulls Wally took long walks along the beach collecting oval-shaped sandstones. Working at night by Coleman lantern, Wally painted filigree designs on the stones he had collected along the beach. He gave me one of his hand-painted stones with the word MERDE (French slang for "shit") filigreed on one side, a souvenir of "the world's greatest goatfuck."

One Step Forward

MiGs, Cubans, and Stalin's Organs, backhanded Soviet responses to Uhuru, an operation beginning to stick in their craw. Even with FLA reverses at Ambrizio, the project was making progress. The *Christina*, fitted out with a Gatling gun and maritime mortar, was preparing for a hit-and-run operation against a Russian supply ship. Castillo and Bentavo, now attached to Uhuru, had recruited and trained two hundred commandos, who would soon be sent in against PMFA and Cuban targets behind the lines.

Sanchez had set up a provisional government, consolidated UTIA's control over the Benguela Railroad, coffee and rubber plantations, and the gold and diamond mines. A third of the country was in the hands of the UTIA.

And Radio Free Angafula was readying the population for the creation of a united front against the communists.

Two Steps Backward

They were now only bizarre playing-pieces in an interminable game, of which he ended up forgetting the rules, who his opponent was, and what the stake was.

—GEORGES PEREC, *Life: A User's Manual*

Although the U.S. "imperialists" had been pilloried in the press for their support of mercenaries and anticommunist independence groups in Angafula, most of the adverse publicity had subsided. Then two Bongo misadventures, not of

Uhuru's making, backfired and ignited another flurry of bad press about our activities in Angafula.

The first misadventure was Bongo's attempt to capture the oil rich enclave, Cabrola.

Cabrola

Cabrola is a part of Angafula that juts into the territory of its covetous neighbor, Buwana. The size of the enclave belies its importance, its rich offshore oil deposits providing the primary source of Angafula's revenue. An American company had offshore drilling rights in Cabrola, its wells pumping out 150,000 barrels per day, providing the government in Lunda $500 million a year in revenues, a large portion of which went to support the Soviet-backed PMFA.

It was a strange twist for an American oil company to be the primary provider for a Soviet-backed organization dedicated to bringing down two anticommunist groups backed by the United States.

The irony wasn't lost on the national security adviser, who tried persuading the chairman of the American oil company to suspend royalties to the government in Lunda. The chairman refused, citing U.S. President Calvin Coolidge's maxim, "The business of America is business."

Cabrola had always been a thorn in the side of President Bongo, and its lucrative offshore oil revenues offered a tempting prize. The current unrest and civil war in Angafula led Bongo to believe the time was ripe to make a grab for the enclave. He secretly hired a hundred foreign mercenaries, many of them ex-members of Major Mike's mercenary battalion, to capture Cabrola. If the raid succeeded as planned, Bongo would step in and claim the enclave for Buwana.

It all went badly awry, and the raid was a fiasco. The operation to capture Cabrola leaked, and Cuban reinforcements were rushed in to shore up the enclave. When the mercenaries attacked, the Cubans were ready. They routed the surprised mercenaries before they had even penetrated the outer perimeter and took a number of prisoners.

The "imperialist lackeys" were put on display at a press conference in Cabrola's capital. Pointing to the prisoners, the governor called the attack "another example of interference in Angafula by the Bongo-American clique." To emphasize his point, he held up a fistful of U.S. dollars seized from the mercenaries.

The second step backward came three months later when President Bongo, still smarting from the Cabrola misadventure, decided to send his two "elite" parachute battalions into southern Angafula to relieve Rebello's forces besieged in Ambrizio. The "invasion" was short-lived and another disaster. The two battalions penetrated less than fifteen miles into Anaconda when they came under a barrage from the Stalin's Organs. Bongo's "elite" battalions immediately turned tail and beat a retreat back to Buwana, slowing only long enough to plunder and pillage Angafulan villages along the way.

The international press once again vilified Bongo, the "CIA puppet," for his unprovoked invasion of a friendly African neighbor.

Although Uhuru played no part in Bongo's disastrous forays into Angafula, the unfavorable publicity tarred Uhuru by association and began the unraveling of the project. An American senator did the rest.

The Bells Toll

A perfect tragedy is the noblest production of human nature.
—JOSEPH ADDISON, *The Spectator*

He was a senior U.S. senator from the Midwest and cochairman of the Foreign Affairs Committee. Senator Smothers had become disturbed and unhappy about the "secret war" in Angafula. Although he had been briefed on Project Uhuru, the senator believed his committee was being kept in the dark about the true extent of U.S. involvement in Angafula.

Senator Richards, chairman of a subcommittee on Africa, shared Smother's misgivings and went on a fact-finding mission to Angafula and Buwana. The senator was accompanied by his aide, a UCLA graduate who had majored in African poetry and was ardent admirer of poet laureate and PMFA president, Augustus Sappho.

The senator and his aide were warmly received in Angafula by Sappho, who arranged for their accommodations. He spoke to them at length about his movement and his aspiration for independence. The gracious host also arranged for them to travel around Angafula, at least in the areas controlled by his PMFA.

Following their visit to Angafula, they went on to Buwana, where the senator asked for a briefing on Agency activities in Angafula. I gave a briefing for the senator and his aide on Uhuru, explaining the origins of the project and its objective to support the two anticommunist independence movements in Angafula.

At this point, the senator's aide broke in to castigate the Agency for supporting two "ultraright" groups instead of Sappho's group of "dedicated freedom fighters." I countered that the "democratic" credentials of Sappho, an alumnus of Moscow's Patrice Lumumba University and leader of an organization bankrolled by the Soviets, were tarnished if not completely discredited. The aide angrily retorted that to run down Sappho just because he studied in Moscow and was friendly with the Russians was as shortsighted as our policy of snubbing Ho Chi Minh for the same reasons.

"And where did that get us? A lost war and an international black eye! Sappho is a poet laureate whose only goal is peace and freedom!"

I interrupted her paean to point out that ten thousand Cuban soldiers and batteries of Soviet rocket launchers were hardly "harbingers of peace and freedom."

The senator broke in to say that during their travels around Angafula, they never saw any Cuban soldiers or Soviet rocket launchers.

It was obvious to me that the senator and his aide had made up their minds about our program in Angafula, probably before they left Washington. The purpose of their trip was simply to validate their conviction that we were involved in an illegal and immoral war in Angafula.

After the briefing, I overheard the senator tell his aide he was going to "shut this war down" when he got back to Washington. The irate senator and his starry-eyed aide were determined to "deep-six" the covert program in Angafula. It was only a matter of time before they would succeed.

Shortly after the senator's visit, the national security adviser arrived in Bintang en route to a conference in Cairo. He asked me to bring him up to date on Uhuru. I gave him a rundown on the escalation of the war. Fidel's troops and batteries of Soviet rocket launchers were pouring into Lunda. Cuban forces were hammering the FLA and preparing a final offensive against Ambrizio. They would then concentrate on Sanchez's UTIA forces, which the Cubans were already probing around in Silvo Porta and Cremona. Unless we could bring in bigger guns or the French Foreign Legion, Uhuru was in trouble. I added that there were some bright spots, however, and told him about the air bridge, the commandos, and our projected maritime operations. Sanchez, now well supplied, was preparing to launch a counteroffensive.

As I began briefing him on the bright spots, I noticed that Heinzleman wasn't really listening. The escalation of the war by the Russians and their Cuban surrogates was to him the writing on the wall, a warning that his plan to thwart the Soviets in Angafula would not be realized. He was also probably aware of the mounting opposition in Congress to the "secret war" in Angafula. I didn't mention the senator's visit and his threat to "shut down" Uhuru, but Heinzleman probably already knew his enemies in Congress couldn't wait to see him fall on his sword.

After I finished briefing Uhuru's architect, Heinzleman and I walked onto the terrace overlooking the river immortalized by Conrad and Stanley. When the rains came, the clumps of water hyacinth would break up and be carried out to sea, where they would, finally disappear, like Uhuru. When we shook hands to say good-bye, I sensed I was no longer in good favor.

Heinzleman was an extraordinary man, a brilliant strategist, and a tough protagonist. He was a strong supporter of covert action, and I felt that somehow in the case of Uhuru, I had let its godfather down. It was not for lack of trying. The blame lay primarily with the Soviets, who didn't have to worry about low profiles, sterilized weapons, or congressional watchdogs.

Ring Down the Curtain

The curtain, a funeral pall,
Comes down with the rush of a storm,
And the angels, all pallid and wan,
Uprising, unveiling, affirm
That the play is the tragedy, "Man"
And its hero the Conqueror Worm.
—EDGAR ALLEN POE, *Ligeia*

Victory has a thousand fathers, defeat is an orphan. The lullaby of Langley when an operation is about to go under.

Senator Smothers had made good on his threat. On December 5, 1975, the Foreign Relations Committee recommended termination of support for the war in Angafula, and an amendment to that effect was subsequently submitted to the Senate. On December 19, by a vote of 54 to 22, the amendment was passed and signed into law by the president.

The curtain had fallen on the Last Covert Action.

The cable advised that Uhuru had been officially terminated. I was to advise Rebello and Sanchez that we could offer them no further support other than a termination bonus for their irregulars. I was instructed to dispose of all Uhuru-related assets, including Land Rovers, printing, generators, and so forth.

I was also ordered to terminate all aircrews and commandos on the Uhuru payroll and to settle property leases with Buwanan landlords.

A clean sweep, fore and aft.

The Curtain Falls

Why . . . better to ring down the curtain before the last act of the play, so that a business that begun so importantly may be saved from so singularly flat a winding-up.
—WILLIAM JAMES, "The Dilemma of Determinism"

I broke the news to Rebello first. The former evangelist was visibly shaken. Recent hammering had taken its toll on his forces, and it was only a matter of time before Ambrizio fell to the Cuban/PMFA forces. Without our support he knew his movement would collapse and his followers would disappear back into their villages.

I passed him the termination bonus and wished him well.

To break the news to Sanchez, I had to go to his base in Cremona, a pictur-esque town on a high plateau with tree-lined boulevards, baroque balustrades, and gothic churches, reminders of their Portuguese colonial heritage.

I had always enjoyed meeting with Sanchez, the former soccer star turned freedom fighter. I could imagine the charismatic bearded figure addressing the UN General Assembly, pointing to his look-alike Castro and lambasting the Cuban leader for sending troops to kill his freedom fighters.

Now I was going to say good-bye and pay him off.

I flew to Cremona on a C-47. The German pilot, Heinze, who flew supply runs into Angafula and Bintang, had made a number of trips to Cremona. He and Sanchez had become friends, and he was sorry to hear this was the last time he would be seeing the UTIA leader.

In Cremona, a driver was waiting in a jeep on the tarmac. As we drove toward Cremona, we passed columns of UTIA troops heading north. When we arrived at Sanchez's compound, it was a beehive of activity, crates being loaded onto trucks, rations and ammunition being passed out to troops assembled in the compound. The UTIA leader had just finished briefing his commanders, who were filing out of UTIA headquarters, leaving behind clouds of blue smoke from Gauloises stumped out in overflowing shell-casings. He came over to meet us, carrying three glasses. After uncorking a bottle of Portuguese wine, he proposed a toast to "friends and freedom." I responded with something about "courage and victory."

Breaking the news to Sanchez wasn't going to be easy.

Sanchez was preoccupied with reports of a Cuban force advancing on Cremona. He estimated that if the reports from his scouts were correct, they would be outside the city in twenty-four hours.

When Sanchez looked at me, I thought for a moment he thought I had come to Cremona as a show of support for the UTIA leader and his beleaguered forces. He quickly reassured me, however. He said he knew why I had come, because he had heard about the congressional amendment on his shortwave radio.

During the evening when we had a chance to talk, I assured Sanchez the amendment was not against UTIA or the FLA. It was a backlash from the Vietnam War. Several senators had convinced their colleagues that the United States was being dragged into another "no-win" war, and the amendment was the result. Unfortunately, the war in Angafula had followed too close on Vietnam.

Sanchez brought out a bottle of brandy, and we talked until midnight. We could hear scattered firing in the distance as Cuban patrols began probing UTIA's defenses. Sanchez advised us to get an early start before the Cubans arrived. He had no inten-tion of trying to defend Cremona and give the Cubans an excuse to destroy the town. He would withdraw and move his forces deep into the interior, where they could reorganize and prepare for a guerrilla campaign against the occupiers.

I wished Sanchez the best of luck and handed him the envelope with our final settlement. He thanked me for all we had done for him and his people: "*Merci,* St. Martin. Please thank the man in the White House and your chief and all the others who have helped us. Tell them the fight isn't over, that we will continue the struggle until Angafula is free.

"*Bonne nuit.*"

When we went to bed, I couldn't drop off to sleep, thinking about Sanchez and his freedom fighters. I was burnt out. Too many unfulfilled commitments, callous terminations, hollow good-byes. I was almost glad it was over.

The Wrecking Crew

The urge for destruction is a creative urge!

—MIKHAIL BAKUNIN

A quick breakfast washed down with a "hair-of-the-dog" coffee laced with cognac, bear hugs from Sanchez, and we were off. The driver made it to the airport in record time, let us out, and roared off. An eerie silence hung over the airport, deserted except for our plane. Heinze climbed into the cockpit and started the engines. Leaving the engines running, he climbed back out of the plane, holding a crowbar in his left hand.

He checked the blocks under the wheels to make sure the plane, its engines vibrating, wouldn't veer off the tarmac. He then jogged toward the terminal, motioning for me to follow. The sliding doors of the terminal entrance were open, and we went inside. The lights were on and the overhead fans were still turning. Heinze grabbed a fire ax off the wall and handed it to me

"Now," he said, "we're going to put this airport out of action, make it Kaput so those Cuban bastards can't use it! Leave the air control and radar devices to me. What I don't take, smash with that ax, and don't leave anything intact!"

I could hear small arms and mortar fire in the distance, and it wouldn't be long before the Cubans made it to the airport. Heinze told me not to worry, because we would be gone before they arrived. I wasn't so sure, but since Heinze was my only way out, I followed him as he climbed up into the tower. Heinze immediately went to work with his crowbar, prying off panels, the air control screen, and radar devices, telling me how much they would bring on the Berlin black market. I began chopping cables, smashing circuit breakers, and breaking out windows.

When Heinze finished disconnecting and prying off the items he was going to take with him, he descended from the tower carrying boxes filled with Texas

Instruments and IBM trophies. By the time he made his last trip to the plane, the tower was a shambles, with shards of broken glass and machine parts littering the tower and lobby.

When Heinze returned from the plane, he went around to the back of the terminal and came back with a gerry can of gasoline. He emptied the contents onto the floor of the terminal, then picked up a rag and soaked it with gasoline. He lit the rag with his Zippo lighter, tossed it on the floor of the terminal, and then we both ran out to the plane.

Heinze climbed into the plane as I kicked away the wheel blocks and climbed in, slamming the door behind me. He finished revving up the engines and taxied down the runway. Then I remembered the Cubans and went up to the cockpit to look out. I could see smoke billowing through the broken windows of the terminal and the tower and could also make out muzzle flashes coming from figures in green uniforms running down the tarmac. When Heinze saw the flashes, he nosed the plane up to get out of range, then banked around and headed north to try to locate Sanchez. When he spotted his column, he dropped down to wag his wings in a final salute. Sanchez looked up and waved, and we headed back to Bintang.

On the way back, Heinze told me the equipment from the tower would bring him almost $50,000 on the black market. I suggested sending part of the proceeds to Sanchez for his war chest, which would soon be depleted. I ran into Heinze almost a year later when I was passing through Frankfurt, and he invited me for a drink at a nearby Bierstube. We spent over an hour reminiscing about that "last flight to Carmona," and at one point I was about to ask him if he had sent a portion of the funds from the airport "fire sale" to Savimbi as I had suggested. Then I remembered the new Porsche parked outside and decided not to ask.

Coup de Grace

The glory that blushed and bloomed
Is but a dim-remembered story
Of the old time entombed.
. . . Vast forms that move fantastically
To a discordant melody;
. . . A hideous throng rush out forever,
And laugh—but smile no more.
—EDGAR ALLEN POE, *Fall of the House of Usher*

It was over. Ambrizio had fallen, and the Cubans had taken Carmona. Uhuru was on its deathbed, but we had no time to administer the last rites. Antennas came down, maps were rolled up, and crates of undelivered M-16s repacked with cosmolene. Portuguese crews and commandos now made redundant sat in bars in Le Cite drinking pastises and wondering where to go next. Fokkers, their logos and altered tail numbers blocked out and repainted, stood forlornly outside Obie's hangar, waiting to be repossessed. The *Christina*, its mortar and Gatling gun removed, had already been stripped by predators. The *De Gama* lay on its side, sand pitted and rusting on the beach near Ambrizio.

The colony of case officers and technicians packed up and returned to Langley. Uhuru's ashes, scattered to the winds wafted over the Kasai savanna or hung over the Goma marshes or floated out to sea.

The Station shrank back to its original size and went back to chasing Russians, scarfing up samples of black-market uranium, and keeping a disgruntled president happy. The only vestiges that remained from the Last Covert Operation were Wally's MERDE rock and shrapnel from a Stalin's Organ.

The Lesson

The Angafulan war had received little attention in the American press, so I was surprised how quickly and with a minimum of debate the Senate had passed the amendment cutting off funds for the Angafulan operation. I learned the reason later.

Several months after Uhuru's termination, a congressional delegation came to Bintang. I had been invited to the ambassador's residence for a reception in the delegation's honor, and while conversing with our defense attaché, I noticed a senator standing alone on the patio smoking a cigar. I walked out to join him and introduced myself. Sam Jackson, senator from Mississippi, held out his hand and said he was glad to meet me.

After an exchange about his trip, the climate and the baseball season in the States, I told the senator I wanted to ask him about something that had been bothering me for some time. Why had the Senate abruptly cut off support for our operation in Angafula? We got out of Vietnam because there was a groundswell of public opinion against the war and mounting American casualties. But Angafula? I'm sure most Americans never heard of the place, and as far as I know, no clamor in the press or public outcry about a covert action operation in a remote corner of Africa. And in Angafula we were supporting the "good guys," two anticommunist groups fighting a pro-communist movement backed by Cuba and the USSR. Why had Congress pulled the plug on our Angafula operation and left the field to the Soviets and Cubans?

The senator puffed on his cigar while he thought about his answer. Then he put his arm around my shoulder, led me to the end of the patio where we were out of earshot, and gave me his answer: "Son, I'm going to give you a civics lesson in how the U.S. Senate works.

Most of a senator's time is spent in his office meeting constituents or on committees hammering out legislation. Now, when a piece of legislation comes out of committee, it goes before the Senate for a vote. A bell rings in the Senate Office Building signaling that a bill is coming up for a vote.

"If it's a 'one bell' call, that means it's a routine piece of legislation coming up for a vote. We usually ignore one-bell calls, because we're busy and the bill probably isn't that important.

"When it's a 'two-bell' call, that means a more important bill is on the floor, and we ought to go cast our vote. We usually respond to two bell calls, but sometimes we are too busy or for some other reason don't make it over to the Capitol to vote, and the bill is passed or voted down with only a minority of the Senate present.

"Now if that bell rings three times, it means a critical piece of legislation is coming up for a vote and we should all get over to the Capitol because every vote counts.

"I remember the three-bell call when that amendment you mentioned came up for a vote. We all piled into that underground train that runs between the Senate Office Building and the Capitol and went over to cast our votes. My aide was standing beside the door leading into the rotunda, waiting to brief me on the legislation up for a vote. He told me there was an amendment on the floor sponsored by Senator Smothers calling for the cutting off of funding for Heinzleman's "secret war" in Angafula, the war he refused to brief the Senate about.

"So, like a lot of other senators, I voted 'yes' and we cut off that secret war. You see, son, a lot of us were mad as hell at that arrogant Prussian [Heinzleman was born in Bavaria, not Prussia] who thought he could stonewall Congress by not briefing us on what his war was all about, how much it was costing, who we were fighting, et cetera. As I said, I voted yes, got Heinzleman, and ended your war!

"Now you may be right and maybe we made a mistake. Most of us knew nothing about Angafula or what the war was all about. I sure as hell didn't know the Russians and the Cubans were in there supplying troops and weapons to a bunch of communists fighting your boys. Maybe if we had been better informed, we wouldn't have been so hasty in voting down the war. We just wanted to let 'The Doctor' know he couldn't cut out Congress and get away with it.

"I'm sorry about your war and that it had to end the way it did. But, son, that's politics!"

End of lesson.

Heinzleman, whose only goal was to deny the Soviets a foothold in Africa, had been hoisted on his petard by a cabal of irate senators.

And Uhuru was left twisting in the wind.

EPILOGUE

Well, I must make a frank confession,
My noon is here, and that's the truth.
So let me with a kind expression
Take leave of my light-hearted youth!
Thank you for all the gifts and fortune,
Thank you for your sorrow and pleasure,
Thank you for sufferings and joys,
For tempests, feasts and noise;
. . . Tomorrow I shall set out brand new ways
And rest myself from earlier days.
　　　　　　　　　—A. PUSHKIN, *Eugene Onegin*

—〰—

Friday was my last day in the Central Intelligence Agency. I had never thought about a "last day," but now it had come.

There were those who would regret my leaving, those still left in that thinning line of covert cadets, recruited when the Agency was young. My departure would remind them that they too, would soon be put out to pasture.

A secretary handed me the box containing the medal I had deliberately left behind in the safe. Medals make a mockery of the spy's covert trademark, anonymity. Next to come would be Nathan Hale Day parades and case officers, in cloak-and-dagger finery, passing in review.

I put the medal in the box with other operational mementos: a "Cosmos Command" plaque from the Saigon bar that sheltered us from a Viet Cong car bomb, an autographed picture of General Ouane, agent of influence now like me, hors de combat; the piece of shrapnel from a Stalin's Organ; a leopard skin toque from Bongo, and Wally's MERDE rock.

My files had been shredded. I walked down the corridor to the rotunda, taking care not to step on "The Truth Shall Set You Free" mosaic. All that was left was to hand my badge to the guard.

I turned in my badge and was heading toward the revolving door when I remembered the capsule, the "quick-fix" elixir in my rear molar to ensure a silent departure before the "long sleep." Working my fingernail under the gold crown, I pried out the "L" tablet. I looked at the pill in my palm, rolled it between my fingers, and flipped it toward an ashtray that stood upright next to the wall. My aim was bad, and the pill ricocheted off the ashtray and dropped onto the tile mosaic.

A cockroach that resembled the cafards that populated the bars of Saigon emerged from a crack at the bottom of the wall. The cafard stood still as its antennae swept the rotunda, finally homing in on the white capsule lying on the mosaic.

Keeping its target in sight, the cockroach, its six legs marching in cadence, made its way across the mosaic toward the capsule. When it reached the "L" pill, its pincers opened wide and like tongs grappling for prizes in a penny arcade game, clamped onto the capsule, ripping it open, the white powder spilling onto the mosaic.

Using its tentacles as chopsticks, the cafard began popping the white grains into an orifice concealed behind its black armored helmet. When it had its fill, it turned around and began to march back across the mosaic toward the crack in the wall.

The cafard never made it. Halfway across the rotunda the cadence of the cockroach slowed and it began reeling drunkenly from side to side. Finally, it collapsed and rolled over on its back, its six legs twitching in the air until rigor mortis kicked in and the twitching stopped.

Le cafard had bought the farm.

I nodded to the bust of Nathan Hale and went out into the cold.

> Shall it be my lot to go that way again,
> I may give those that desire it a full account
> Of what I am here silent about.
> Meantime I bid my reader adieu.
> As for me, my work ends here.
> Let another deal with what comes next.
>
> —XENOPHON

Respectfully submitted,
Stuart Methven, Case Officer

> Good-bye, my book! Like mortal eyes, imagined ones must close some day. And yet the ear cannot right now part with the music and allow the tale to fade, the chords of fate itself continue to vibrate; and no obstruction for the sage exists where I have put, The End.
>
> —VLADIMIR NABOKOV, *The Gift*

INDEX

—⟋⟍—

ABOUT THE AUTHOR

—⚎—

Stuart Methven was born in Honolulu, Hawaii, in 1927. He attended Lenox Preparatory School in Lenox, Massachusetts, and served in the U.S. Army from 1945 to 1947, during the early occupation of Germany. From 1947 to 1951 he attended Amherst College, Amherst, Massachusetts, earning a bachelor's degree in history in 1951. He later attended the Massachusetts Institute of Technology, earning a master's degree in international affairs. From 1951 to 1978 Methven was an operations officer for the Central Intelligence Agency, serving in a variety of posts, mainly in Asia. From 1982 to 1984 he was the owner, publisher, and editor of the *Martinsburg News*, a weekly newspaper in Martinsburg, West Virginia. From 1985 to 1986 he served as a representative and consultant on matters related to Europe, Africa, and the Middle East for the Hudson Institute. From 1987 to 1988 Methven was assistant to the president of the Center for Naval Analyses. He lives in Brussels, Belgium.

The Naval Institute Press is the book-publishing arm of the U.S. Naval Institute, a private, nonprofit, membership society for sea service professionals and others who share an interest in naval and maritime affairs. Established in 1873 at the U.S. Naval Academy in Annapolis, Maryland, where its offices remain today, the Naval Institute has members worldwide.

Members of the Naval Institute support the education programs of the society and receive the influential monthly magazine *Proceedings* or the colorful bimonthly magazine *Naval History* and discounts on fine nautical prints and on ship and aircraft photos. They also have access to the transcripts of the Institute's Oral History Program and get discounted admission to any of the Institute-sponsored seminars offered around the country.

The Naval Institute's book-publishing program, begun in 1898 with basic guides to naval practices, has broadened its scope to include books of more general interest. Now the Naval Institute Press publishes about seventy titles each year, ranging from how-to books on boating and navigation to battle histories, biographies, ship and aircraft guides, and novels. Institute members receive significant discounts on the Press's more than eight hundred books in print.

Full-time students are eligible for special half-price membership rates. Life memberships are also available.

For a free catalog describing Naval Institute Press books currently available, and for further information about joining the U.S. Naval Institute, please write to:

Member Services
U.S. Naval Institute
291 Wood Road
Annapolis, MD 21402-5034
Telephone: (800) 233-8764
Fax: (410) 571-1703
Web address: www.usni.org